45

TIPS, TRICKS, AND SECRETS FOR THE SUCCESFUL IB STUDENT

TIPS, TRICKS, AND SECRETS FOR THE SUCCESFUL IB STUDENT

ALEXANDER ZOUEV

ZOUEV PUBLISHING

Copyright © 2017 Alexander Zouev. All rights reserved.

Published 2017
Printed by Lightning Source

ISBN 978-0-9934187-8-5, paperback.

Dedicated to you, the student.

Introduction

Before we dive into the substantive part of this guidebook, I wish to spend a few pages explaining who I am, and my motivation for compiling and writing this book. This is not my first IB guidebook, but it will (hopefully) be my last, in the sense that I wish to exhaust every piece of crucial advice that I have. I hope that this endeavour will be more structured and reflective than my previous IB guidebooks, and I certainly hope it reaches and helps as many students.

Before diving into the world I like to call "stress-free IB" you may want to ask yourself the question "who am I to listen to some stranger's advice on how to do well on my IB?" At least I hope you are asking yourself this question. After all, I have never officially worked at an IB school, nor am I in any way affiliated with the organisation. Moreover, in recent years, the market for IB 'help' material has become greatly saturated with both recommendable and also some avoidable books being published. Thus before going into the details of how to maximize your IB points total, let me put your mind at ease by providing a little background on myself and my own academic experiences.

I graduated with the International Baccalaureate Diploma Program totalling 43 points in 2007, setting a school record at the time and finishing top in most of my classes. The next few years were spent at Oxford University where I completed my BA in Economics and Management, while simultaneously starting to tutor students over Skype from my dorm room. It was during the summer breaks of these years that I completed by first IB guidebook, *Three*, which dealt with the 3 'bonus point' (Extended Essay and Theory of Knowledge) component of the diploma.

Upon graduating from Oxford, I pursued an MSc in Financial Mathematics from the Cass Business School in London. During this year, I completed my second IB guidebook, *I Think Therefore IB*, which incidentally serves as the inspiration for this book. It was around this time that I was also one of the first tutors to work for EliteIB (www.eliteib.co.uk) which has now grown to be one of the largest IB tutoring agencies in the world.

I left EliteIB to set up my own freelancer IB tutoring practice – IBTutorOnline (www.ibtutoronline.com). It was here that I honed my skills as an Economics and Mathematics tutor, specializing in helping students with their Internal Assessments. I was busy with IBTutorOnline for over five years and in that time oversaw hundreds of Extend Essays, TOK assignments, and helped over 200 students in their IB studies. My students improved their grades, on average, by 2.3 points and I even had the pleasure of tutoring several 45/45 students.

In 2015, I set up a small publishing house (www.zouevpublishing.com) that specializes in publishing IB guidebooks, written by former students and aimed at current students. We have published books that cover subjects such as History and Physics, as well as general IB guidebooks. I also developed a smartphone app aimed directly at IBDP candidates – smartib (www.smartibapp.com).

This app is a social media platform and community forum app designed specifically for students undergoing the IBD program. The app allows students to create a profile and connect with other IB students all over the world via a well-organised forum where they can ask and answer questions. In the first three months, we have over 8,000 registered users who are using the app on a daily basis to meet other students and help each other out. I'm very hopeful that this app is going to make a lot of differences to students who aren't lucky enough to have the best teachers and resources at their disposal.

So, basically, over the last 10 years I have become somewhat of a Mr. IB (as my friends jokingly call me). I have been an active contributor on IB forums, and I have probably personally and directly helped nearly 1000 IB students over all the years. I truly believe that as far as being a consultant on the broader IB goals of achieving success, I am probably the best at what I do – which leads us to the creation of this book.

Reading this book is probably the most efficient method of earning a 40+ grade in your International Baccalaureate Diploma. Whether you are a student in need of guidance, a teacher looking to find new teaching techniques, or simply an interested reader – hopefully you will find that this extensive treasure-chest of advice meets all of your expectations. If you follow the advice put forth in this book correctly and put in some effort and determination, I firmly believe that you can obtain a points total of 40 or above – irrespective of any 'natural' intelligence.

Those of you still curious to know, the two points I missed out on to get a 45 where due to a 6 in Physics (Standard Level) and a 6 in English (Standard Level). Looking back I do blame myself for not following my own advice enough to get that 7 in Physics, however the English I have no regrets about; I tried my best and did what I could, but did not get a 7. Unfortunately, and despite the title, this book will not teach you how to get a perfect score of 45/45 and place you into the top 0.01% of candidates. I know plenty of people who have obtained this amazing feat; however, almost all admit to having had a slice of good fortune somewhere along their path to perfection. With most university offers capped at around 40 points, there is also no need to get a perfect score - unless you are the ultimate perfectionist.

There is no effortless way to achieve the grades that you want. There are however ways that will save you time, effort, and money, yet still let you reach your maximum potential and get the grades you dream of. For those of you reading to find any tips on plagiarism, cheating or any other non-ethical method to get a higher grades, you will have to look elsewhere. My tips and techniques are 100% in line with the rules and regulations of the IB guidelines. Understandably, there will be critics amongst parents and teachers who suggest that a lot of what I endorse is in some ways non-ethical and not in accordance with what the IB preaches. These arguments lack merit. Countless students are getting the top grades and succeeding without actually succumbing to becoming lifeless bookworms. One needs to understand and appreciate that there is "cheating" and then there are "tactical and efficient study techniques", and there is a thick line separating the two concepts. This book will ultimately teach you to become masters of manipulating the resources at your disposal efficiently and tactically, without having to resort to anything that can be regarded as 'cheating'.

What is essential before we begin is that you throw away all preconceived notions about the IB as being something scary, elitist, incredibly demanding and impossible to crack. I was once amongst you, but after finding out that the IB is just as easy to decipher as the A-levels, the AP programs, or the SATs – I became fearless. This is an essential stepping-stone in your long road to IB success. Yes, your non-IB friends will call you an overachieving geek. Yes, you may find you have more assignments and tests than the other "normal" kids. And yes, there will be times when you wonder why your parents/teachers would ever want to put you through so much traumatising pain. However, one should not fear. The techniques in this book will ensure that your two-year ride in the IBDP will be amongst the most memorable and fun two years of your life.

It certainly was for me.

1. Is the IB For Me?

Before you even embark on your IB adventure, you need to decide if the IB is for you. By that I mean, is the IB diploma the bridge you need to get to the next point in your life – whatever that may be?

Depending on where you are located geographically, what your future career ambitions are, and what school choices are on offer, you may be faced with the task of deciding whether the IB is worth it in your individual situation. Let's start by briefly looking exactly what the IB Diploma Program entails:

Founded nearly 50 years ago, the IB organization is a non-profit institution that offers an international education to students at over 3,500 IB World schools in 145 countries. The Diploma Program includes an advanced academic curriculum and several core requirements, including the Extended Essay (a kind of senior thesis), Theory of Knowledge (an epistemology course that emphasizes the IB philosophy), and CAS (extracurricular activities highlighting "creativity, action, and service" that counterbalance academic studies). Your IB final examination scores and fulfilment of above requirements determine whether you earn the IB diploma.

If that sounds like a lot of work – it's because it is. There is a good reason that the IB program has such a notoriously difficult and rigorous reputation around the world. The upside is that you are encouraged to think independently and learn how to think. You also become more culturally aware as you develop a second language, and you will be able to engage with people in an increasingly globalized and rapidly changing world.

US Scenario

It's widely considered that American students rarely take on the IB diploma to attend university outside of the States, but rather to earn as many college-transferable credits as possible (to "get ahead" in completing General Education requirements in college) or increase their college application marketability by boasting the IB diploma as an achievement on their resume.

Advanced Placement courses have long been considered the go-to option for U.S. high schoolers who desire more challenging work than what's offered in the standard curriculum. But IB students may have more options for getting an academic challenge. An increasing number of American high schools offer the IB program which, like the AP program, offers a rigorous set of courses. Moreover, the SATs and your GPA seem to still be the dominant factors which US universities look at when deciding on applicants. Thus, it would make sense for US-based students to find out if their 'dream' university will be more likely possible if they take the IB. This could even mean you need to call up the universities and talk to their admissions offices.

More importantly, students can earn college credits by taking certain IB subjects. This is very important to consider because rather than taking the full diploma, you may be inclined to take IB certificates instead. If a student chooses to pursue the IB certificate route and not the full lB Diploma he/she does not have to complete the Theory of Knowledge course, the Extended Essay, or the 150 hours over two years of CAS. Taking IB Certificates is similar to taking AP courses. Those students enrolled as just certificate students could also choose to take the AP tests and, therefore, double dip with IB and AP credit on their transcript.

There is also the cost to consider: IB exams are more expensive than AP. There is a $160 registration fee each year plus $110 fee per exam. AP exams are 92$ without an additional fee. Many schools however have financial aid and fee-waiver programs. If financing is an issue for you, you should contact your school and see if help is available. Talk with a counsellor at your school to find out about testing costs.

I know it seems crazy to be thinking about all of this when you are 15 years old and don't even know much about university and what you wish to study, but the IB is a huge decision and one you should not take lightly. The main advice here is to do your research. I can only give general help, each case will vary on the specifics, so pick up that phone and start calling potential universities to find out their recognition of the IB Diploma.

UK Scenario

In the UK (and some parts of Europe), the choice is altogether different. Here you are required to choose between the traditional A-levels and the IB. Although the IB has only been around since 1968, it has grown substantially in the UK and is finding itself offered at more schools, often alongside the A-levels.

If your school offers both, then it's relatively agreed upon which students do more work. Over the two years, IB students will get up to half as much teaching as their A-level counterparts. On top of that, they have to adopt a more inquiring approach than A-level students. There is also this myth that because IB students can only do two sciences (and A-level students could potentially do three), they have less chance of getting into medical school. This has been proven false as IB students are as successful (if not more) and the IB lets students do biology and chemistry (which is essential for medicine) alongside maths.

Prospective IB students should take comfort in the fact that the IB has become more and more appreciated by UK universities. As a rule of thumb, an IB score of 7 earns 130

UCAS points, while an A* is worth 140 points, and an A-grade 120.

Arguments for students opting for A-levels instead of IB usually focus around the principle objection that the IB lumbers students with subjects which they may have no interest or aptitude for. The A-level system allows students who aren't very good at maths, or hate languages, to abandon these weaknesses once their GCSEs are over – but the IB requires you take on these challenges for two more years.

Rest of the World

Non-US/UK students face different scenarios altogether. I can't possibly go into the details for each individual country, but basically it boils down to what choices you have on offer in your national education system, and where you wish to go once you finish high school. I have met plenty of students who wanted to go straight into a trade job once completing high school, or someone who wanted to enter the family business as soon as possible. In these situations, I can understand why the two years of the IB Diploma would seem like a time waste.

Ultimately (and I may be slightly biased in this assessment) the IB Diploma does in fact develop well-rounded, inquisitive and global learners. I would strongly argue that it's the best high school education a student can get, and it opens the door to so many diverse opportunities. The skillset you acquire upon completion of the program is going to set you up for a very successful future career.

The IB Diploma is not for everyone. Although it is a wonderfully challenging program that has gained incredible worldwide recognition, you need to look at your individual scenario and decide if it the program is right for you and for where you want to be in a few years.

2. IB vs AP

(contributed article)

Due to the rising popularity of the IB program in the America, we decided to include a specific chapter to deal with how US-based students should approach their IB (as most of the information available caters to European audiences).

It's true, the International Baccalaureate Diploma Program is daunting. Certainly, a formidable opponent, monstrous with its intent on obstructing your journey to a happier destination. Coming from a less-than-adequately-funded school in urban America, I've seen quite a few of my friends shrink away at the thought of tackling the academic juggernaut. However, like most of life, the greater the challenge, the greater the reward. I can't speak with authority on universities outside of the United States, though I'm sure they're quite similar, but I can assure you that the most prestigious American universities look upon an International Baccalaureate Diploma with immense respect and appreciation.

Some context for you: my high school was and is the poorest public educational facility in the immediate district and most of the surrounding area. It also happens to be the most diverse school in the entire state of Washington with over 65 languages spoken, about as international as it gets here in America. More than 60% of the student body receives financial aid in the form of "free or reduced lunch". The school offers only 15 International Baccalaureate classes, 8 of which are Standard Level only and many of which were only added within the past year. This contrasts with the 40+ subjects provided by the Programme, the clear majority of which are available in both Standard and Higher Level.

With all that in mind please trust me when I say, within reason, everybody willing to put in the effort can graduate the Programme with flying colors.

A very good friend of mine, illegal immigrant and from a poor backrgound, was accepted into a Top 20 American university with a full ride scholarship, all thanks to the International Baccalaureate Diploma Programme. Your two years in this esteemed Programme will be hellish. You will stress, you will question your decision and yes, you will consider dropping out. But your two years in this Programme will be worth it. It will prepare you for university, it will prepare you for your career and yes, it will prepare you for your future. So why Choose IB over AP?

1) Preparation for College

Though it may be true that AP Students get much more college credit than their fellow IB counterparts, the IB does infinitely more in preparing you for the workload you will receive in college. What makes the IB such a daunting program is the fact that it throws so much information at you. Students that do well in the IB can effectively manage this information, learn it efficiently, and at the same time maintain healthy, balanced lives. In college, similarly, you're going to be bombarded with all kinds of information, both academic and non-academic. You're going to have to make choices on prioritizing your work over going to a frat party, about whether you can afford to join another extracurricular activity, or whether staying up all night to finish that paper is worth it. In this sense, the IB offers you invaluable experience and you should treat everything it throws at you as a learning curve for college. Last time I checked, AP students didn't have to write a 4000-word research paper, question their own existence, and manage CAS activities whilst having to juggle six subjects. Truth be told, the IB will make the college transition very smooth and you'll go in feeling like a rockstar.

2) Broader Perspective

Let's be honest: The APs have always been primarily geared to provide an American Education, possessing very few courses such as AP Word History that critically examine society from a global perspective. Before I get bullets fired at me for challenging the greatest nation in the world, let me add that this is completely fine: The APs prepare you very well for college and ensure you learn loads of material. However, I personally feel the IB offers you something much more rich and substantial. Indeed, the IB turns you into a scholar of the world: you're forced to examine things from multiple different perspectives, challenge assumptions, and this leads you to become a well-rounded, critical thinker. Sure, you can argue that this global mumbo-jumbo isn't necessary, and that the point of a high-school program should be to simply gain knowledge in subjects you're interested (hence why you don't have as many subjects if you do the APs). But the way I see it, the IB is in a way that 'study abroad' experience that so many people claim is invaluable. Think of yourself as Dora the Explorer, always questioning everything around you, and wanting to delve further into your intellectual pursuits.

3) Alumni Love

This doesn't seem like a real reason, but hear me out. Nothing quite compares to being in college, meeting someone new, and then realizing that both of you are IB Alumni! You suddenly feel as if you have known each other for many, many years and can relate to each other. The pain, the misery, the grade boundaries—oh, what bliss! It's like you're family. No, you ARE family.

4) Creativity, Action, Swag

Though the IB is a lot of work, it ensures that you pursue worthwhile and enjoyable activities outside the classroom. You're going to graduate highschool having done activities that you previously would never have thought of doing, and the most exciting part is that one of these activities might end up being something you love to do! Take it from me: I unwillingly decided to learn chess to fulfil my Creativity Section, after my mother went out and spent money on buying a chess board. Hundreds of hours later, chess has become one of my favourite hobbies, one that I pursue even in college! See, the AP Program aims to simply focus on the courses that you take. The IB, as hard as it may sound to believe, wants you to go outside and discover the amazing opportunities that are available.

5) Work Ethic

Granted, the average IB student will have more work to do than the average AP student. You take more subjects, have a lot to do outside the classroom, and oh god, there's just so much writing to do! But whilst doing all of this, you start to develop a strong work ethic. Even if you procrastinate, you realize that you just must get your work done. Unless you want very little sleep, you start to become much more efficient with your work and know how to prioritize your day. You know whether you can afford to go out with your friends, or should rather stay in to do some revision. Conversely, you realize that having a social life is also important to maintaining a balanced lifestyle, and thus you make time to hang out with your friends. These are invaluable skills not only to hone for college, but also for the rest of your life. With each day, you start to work smarter, you start to feel like a champion.

6) Research and Investigation Skills

If you've ever been interested in doing research (or even if you haven't) the IB is an excellent program to cultivate investigative qualities. The IAs that you must write for your sciences ensure that you develop skills in data analysis, know how to work with uncertainties, and are comfortable combining both quantitative and qualitative elements to form a cogent paper. The Internal Assessments that you must write for your Humanities, especially Economics, allow you to combine real-life information and theory to craft a compelling argument. The Math Internal Assessment is an amazing way to understand the practicalities of Math in the real world, and allow you to consolidate your fundamentals in specific areas. The Extended Essay that you must write gives you real-hand experience on drafting a paper of such large volume. And of course, who can forget scourging the Internet for all those precious past papers and their markschemes.

7) A Powerful Resume

Think about if for a second. In a world where colleges expect you to do a billion activities, ask you to go above and beyond both within and outside the classroom, and even want you to do research, isn't the IB marvellous? Your CAS lead to all those Extra-Curricular Activities, you get to put down your EE as 'research' (I for sure did), and your TOK endeavours demonstrate intellectual curiosity. Aren't you, by simply doing the IB, building up an awesome portfolio for applying to college? All the stuff that you learn, that you do, and that you're able to get deeply involved in will look fantastic on your application, for both college and prospective internships.

8) Way of Thinking vs Curriculum Readiness

The APs will ensure that once you get to college, you know the curriculum that is going to be covered and that you've had some sort of experience dealing with it beforehand. That's in part why the AP Program warrants so many college credits. However, what the IB program will do is that it will force you to develop a dynamic way of thinking that is tailored to new situations. That is, you may not have seen the material presented to you, but you will be fantastically equipped to deal with it. You will recognize patterns, structure your revision effectively, look at details from different perspectives; essentially, you'll have a mental toolkit ready to tackle all sorts of new problems. To me, that's something that is much more important than simply gaining enough college credits or having familiarity with the curriculum. Life is all about adapting to new situations, solving new problems, and the IB is what is going to prepare you for the best.

3. Irrational IB Fear

Perhaps one of the first and most important topic to address is this widespread belief that the IB programme is elitist, unrealistically difficult, and a two-year burden on your teenage life. You need to throw away all your negative preconceptions and fears about the IB diploma and start believing in yourself. No matter who you are and what kind of academic record you have had up to this point in your life, the IB diploma program is an opportunity for you to start anew.

I have known students that have come from C grade averages to end up with high 30s on their IB diploma. I was quite the high-school slacker and troublemaker until I realised that my IB grades could decide a large part of my near future. The key here is that natural intelligence and 'book-smart' are not essential to achieving IB success. What is essential however is the willpower and self-belief that you can survive and succeed in the most academically intense high school degree program and come out with flying colours.

Consider your two-year IB experience as something of a sporting event. The final exams are the grand finale, and everything before is your preparation and training for that event. I use this sporting analogy because it highlights the importance of planning and mental preparedness that is needed to perform at the highest level. Even the greatest athletes cannot do their best unless they master the skill of visualizing their own success.

Without getting too philosophical, I do want to stress how important this 'visualization' exercise is. Unless you can imagine yourself getting the top marks and achieving a total of 40+ points, it will be very difficult to do so in reality. This is not a 'self-help' book per se, nor do I fully agree with the ideas that some self-help books tend to promote – most famously The Secret's notion that anything is possible if you keep thinking about it. However, although I don't think that visualization alone is sufficient for success, I do think that it is necessary.

When someone tells you that the IB program is 'difficult', you need to appreciate that difficulty is always relative. Yes, perhaps compared to the A-Levels or the AP program, the IB is more academically challenging and there is more work to be done. However, this does not mean that the IB is the hardest task any 16-18 year olds across the world must face. Trust me, there will be much more demanding and stressful challenges as you get older. Don't let this 'IB fear' become a scapegoat for underperformance. I see this happen all the time. Students get lost in this illusion of the IB as something impossible, and subsequently lose any motivation to do well because they think it is beyond their reach. This is where mental strength is of upmost importance.

The first few weeks of the IB program are relatively tranquil. Use this 'easing-in' period as an opportunity to prove to yourself that you can conquer and beat anything the IB program throws at you. Only once you overcome your mental fear of the IB program can you begin to deal with the challenges of the program itself. It is imperative that your first few weeks of the program go as smooth as possible. If you start to fall behind early, any preconceived fears you may have had will soon turn into a reality. So at least for the first month or so make sure you meet all of the deadlines and perform at your highest level. Once you have proven to yourself that you can overcome the first month, any fear left will gradually dissolve.

Now that we've got the fear aspect out of the way, the question becomes: how should you best spend the few months leading up to your first day in the IB program? Unfortunately, there is no concrete answer, and you will hear a variety of responses when asking who have been through it all. However, there are certainly some things you can do that are more beneficial than others.

Summer time is here and you must relax, so for a few weeks forget that you are even in the IB. I suggest doing this in the start of summer. I also strongly recommend travelling and relaxing with friends and family. Take this as an opportunity to reset, and go fresh into the IB next year.

Now say 3-2weeks are left before the IB starts or restarts, what do you do? You get back to work and you work hard! Ok, but what do you work on? Firstly, be sure that there is nothing you don't understand from the previous year. Make sure to patch up all your weak points. If there is something you don't understand in Chemistry, go over it, review it and then test yourself.

Do not be afraid to send a few emails to your teachers, they will find it incredible that you are working during you summer. If you have also noticed that you are not good at a particular type of assignment, for example you seem to score poorly on certain types of English essays, research into them, rewrite a few essays and then ask your teacher to look over them.

Say you have patched up all your areas of weakness, what now? It's time to get ahead of the game. Look over the assignments you will have to do next year and start preparing for those. If you can't do that, then look over certain particularly difficult topics you will be doing next year and go over them. In all honesty you will probably not have much time to get ahead, most of your 2-3weeks will be consumed with review work and patching any weakness in your knowledge. On that note, enjoy the summer and best of luck to you.

4. Subject Choice [Part I]

Although to most of you this chapter will have little relevance, to those who are yet to decide which subjects you want to take – this chapter is of great importance. I find that choosing your subjects is, rather unfortunately, underestimated in importance. You are deciding what you will learn in depth for the next two years of your life. So, just as you would take time to choose a college degree, an occupation or a spouse, you should sit down and think about what interests you - even slightly. There are a few factors that you should consider and I have outlined these below:

Interest

As with almost everything you do, you will tend to succeed more and find it easier if you are doing something you have an interest for and enjoy. The same goes for IB subjects. Although this is of less importance in choosing a group 1 or 2 language, it has great importance in choosing your group 4 science and group 3 subject. If you know for a fact that you have absolutely no passion and interest for memorizing human anatomy and studying Biology, then you can cross that off. If, on the other hand, you want your IB to have as little maths as possible, then you probably would not be too interested in studying Physics. If you are strongly passionate about a certain subject and are already reading external material concerned with it, then by all means go ahead and take it into consideration.

However, one should be careful not to confuse interest with vague curiosity. If you always thought that graffiti is cool, it would not be wise choosing HL Visual Art solely based on that observation. Similarly, don't let a childhood obsession with spaceships be the deciding factor for choosing HL Physics. This is where a slight familiarity with the course content can greatly help. Take the time to glance over the syllabus of the course you are interested in, and only then check to see if it matches your interests.

Ability

Obviously if you are clearly naturally gifted in a certain subject then you should thank your natural abilities and take it. Of course, there are limitations to this rule of thumb. I used to be obsessed with drawing and graphic design, and for many years believed I would be studying Art at Diploma level. However, as the time came for me to make my final decision, I did a little research (with the statistics that the IB provides on their webpage) and talked to many seniors who had previously done Art as a subject. The general feeling seemed to be that if I wanted to go for a subject that I enjoyed, excelled at, and wouldn't be under too much stress then I should choose Art instead of another Group 3 topic. Having done that research also showed me that it seemed very few get 7s in Art (especially in my school), no matter how passionate or how good the candidate is (perhaps due to the nature of the final exam and luck of the draw).

Since I was more concerned with obtaining a 7 than following my passion for Art and gambling with the grade, I chose geography (which I also had a reasonable ability for). The message I'm trying to get across is that often students get confused about how great their abilities are in a certain subject. Just because you got A's in English in Elementary School does not mean that you should expect to jump into a Higher Level English exam and effortlessly produce a grade 7 piece of work. Be honest with yourself when assessing your own ability in a certain subject.

Future

Please don't get me wrong. When I say future I don't mean that the subjects you choose for your IB diploma will reflect in any way where you will be in ten years and what sort of occupation you will have (although, funnily enough, they have for me). Nevertheless, you do need to take into consideration what you want to do at university level if you plan on pursuing a university education. It's unfortunate that you need to be thinking about your post-school decision from almost the age of 16 when university is probably the last thing on your mind but that's the reality of it. Too often I have seen students wanting to study medicine at a top UK university be rejected because, despite taking Biology as a subject, they did not take Chemistry, which is often a requirement to study medical science. The same can be said for students wanting to study Economics. Taking Mathematics Studies severely limits your chances of ending up a at a top Economics course – in most cases.

Thus, if you're one of those students that has his/her heart set on a specific course at a specific university by the age of 16, then you should do some research and find out which courses are essential, and which will help you in getting closer to your goal. For those of you thinking of studying abroad, you may want to reconsider which foreign languages you want to take, if your school offers a wider variety.

Although this is important to take into consideration, don't worry too much about it. In most cases offers from universities are given based on a final score, rather than subject-specific. Also, I have seen people go on to get PhDs in Economics without having taken Economics as an IB subject. So, with regards to the long-term future, subject choice is probably not the most important factor to consider.

Teachers

This is a tough one. I hate to say it but there is such a thing as a "bad teacher" even in the glamorous top-of-the-line world of the IB Diploma. Trust me; I have seen the best of both worlds. Some of the teachers I have worked with were masters at what they did, with more than a decade of first-hand IB experience. Then there were those who probably couldn't spell International Baccalaureate – let alone teach it.

Most students tend to believe this idea where the teacher is the one factor that will make or break the subject. They think that the teacher has a greater influence on the final grade than they do themselves.

I do not agree. Even if your teacher is utterly useless at what they are hired to do, this does not mean you should spend two years moaning only to ultimately fail the subject and live your whole life cursing that teacher. Believe me, I have seen some of the worst of the worst. But even despite the poor teaching I've seen students get past that and take matters into their own hands to come out with a grade they truly deserve. Yes, it's true, if you have a poor teacher then you will spend most of your time becoming best friends with the subject textbooks. But let's be honest here, we don't live in a perfect world, hence we don't all have world class IB teachers.

With regards to the subject material, you should not have to worry too much if your teacher is clueless. But, when it comes to things such as external assessments and choosing options for examinations, you should ensure that they know what they are talking about. You don't want to sit a two-year program only to find that your teacher messed up the internal assessments you gave in and thus you lose almost 25% of your total mark.

By the time you begin your IB program, you will have heard all the rumours about who is a great IB teacher and who shouldn't even be teaching preschool. Don't completely ignore these. If you're the type of person who simply cannot take matters into their own hands and work independently for most of the year, then by all means look for the "best" and most engaging teachers that are available. If, on the other hand, you don't need to be spoon-fed information that is readily available for you yourself to read from the textbooks, then it shouldn't matter. In this case, you should choose subjects based on the other criteria I have outlined.

5. Subject Choice [Part II]

If you thought that those were the only factors to consider when choosing your courses, well you would be mistaken. The top students also consider some less obvious elements.

School records

If you are one of those students sitting the IB Diploma simply to obtain the highest score possible no matter which subjects then you would be wise to do a little bit of research. Find out how well your school has performed in different subjects over the years. If for the past ten years not a single person has gotten a 7 in Chemistry, then your best bet would probably be not to choose it if you are looking for a 7 in your Group 4 subject. If on the other hand, it has been decades since someone has gotten below a 5 in your school's History SL program, and you are the type of person that would be more than happy with a 5 or above then by all means go for it.

Don't limit this research to your school records alone. Go online and find out which subjects have the greatest fail rates, the greatest number of 7's, and what the median marks are. All of this information is readily available on the IBO website – under the section of 'Statistical Bulletins'. There is an abundance of information in these reports, so take the time to analyse them. I don't encourage making decisions completely based on statistics, but playing the numbers game will not prevent you from making better choices.

Difficulty

There is a myth in the IB world that claims that all IB kids do an equal amount of work, no matter what subjects they choose. Perhaps the phrasing is a bit unclear there. Yes, it can be that the actual amount of work (hours assigned) is the same from subject to subject. Don't be fooled into thinking that each candidate faces the same difficulty. This is especially true because of the IB's system of separating Higher Level and Standard Level subjects.

Take two random students with exactly same subject choices, apart from the fact that student X takes Maths HL and Geography SL, whereas student Y takes Maths Studies (SL) and Geography HL. One would have an incredibly difficult time arguing that the gap in difficulty between Maths SL and HL is the same as the gap between Geography SL and HL. The gap in difficulty between Maths HL and SL is incomparable to the gap in Geography.

There is no point in kidding ourselves. If you want to challenge yourself, then by all means take HL: Economics, Mathematics, English, Physics, SL: History, Language B. If you want to lay back a bit and not be under too much stress and get a guaranteed pass, take HL: Theatre Arts, Geography, Environmental Systems, SL: English, Language (ab initio), and Business Management. Let's be honest here; it's no secret that Physics or Chemistry are academically more demanding than Environmental Systems.

All of this is not something to be ashamed of either. You may opt to take a less stressful route, with a lighter workload – and this is perfectly fine. The point I am trying to make is that you need to figure out what your ultimate aim is. Do you want to choose demanding courses that interest you and will challenge you? Or do not have little interest in what subjects you do as long as you get 35+ by the end of the two years? There is little wrong with either of the choices, but the important thing to remember is that the choice is real and the choice is yours.

Resources

As much as the IB tries to make their students more educated, inquisitive and imaginative, I am often shocked at how little students use the resources available at their disposal. The Internet is an invaluable weapon in your IB survival toolkit. Go online and find out if there are any great books available on your subjects of interest. Find out how long the course has been taught and whether it has been significantly modified in recent years.

Keep in mind that if the resources are scarce for you subject of interest, then it probably means that you will struggle to find help outside your classroom. More well-established subjects have an incredible surplus of information readily available to find on the internet and in books. The newer subjects, or the less popular choices, will undoubtedly have less helpful information.

On a final note, I fully appreciate that there are many students out there crying "my school just launched the IB Diploma program and I don't have a choice of what science to choose because they only offer Chemistry at HL!" Unfortunately, that is just a fact of life. Not a single school will offer all the IB subject choices that are available, so you need to make the best out of the situation. Don't waste your time protesting and making petitions asking your school to introduce a subject that would probably yield high demand from the students. It's much more complicated than that as there are monetary, time and faculty constraints that need to be taken into account.

In certain specific circumstances, however, there are ways in which you can 'create' a new subject for yourself – given your school allows this. You could potentially sit the two years in a HL class only to then undertake the SL exam. This may be frowned upon by your school, but try to see if this is possible. I initially started the IB program with the intention of doing four HL subjects (Economics, Mathematics, Geography and Physics) as opposed to the usual three. However, as the time came to make final exam choices, I realised that I would be better off dropping one of my HLs rather than risking getting a lower grade. Physics HL was

27

unfortunately a bit too demanding for me, and I argued that it took away too much revision time from my other HL subjects in which I was trying to achieve 7s. I repeatedly asked the IB coordinator to be allowed to sit the SL Physics exam, and continue to sit the Physics HL class. Eventually all the details were sorted out and it worked out fine.

I'm not saying sit HL classes for all of your subjects, but this is certainly an overlooked tactic for the more ambitious students out there. If you are not challenged enough and would find it beneficial learning some HL material despite sitting the SL exam then try to make that possible by carefully discussing it with your IB coordinator. Note also that the HL teacher may be much 'better' than the SL one.

There is also the possibility of self-study or following online courses (check the Pamoja online education program). Again, you will need to check this with your school and IB co-ordinator. It is understandable why many schools are wary of external course providers. Also, there is a monetary burden to consider.

At the end of the day the choice of which subjects you will do will largely depend on how the schedule blocks in your school work and what subjects they actually have on offer. Don't make a huge fuss if you can't get exactly what you want. There are thousands of students out there in similar situations – if not worse. Work with what you have. Take my tips listed above, consult your parents, consult your teachers, consult your older school friends and hopefully this will help you reach a decision.

Do not choose a subject "because my friend is doing it as well." This is probably the dumbest thing you can do when it comes to making subject choices. Chances are you and your "friends" will see each other in other classes, and you'll have enough time to hang out outside of class.

Anticipated Subject

An 'Anticipated' subject is just the IB's fancy name for an accelerated subject. When you sign up to study an Anticipated subject, you have about one year to actually finish the entire subject. This means that you will have only 5 subjects to worry about in the last year of IB. But this also means a lot more stress during the first year of IB when you have to cram two years of content into just one year.

Most people's first reaction: What if I can't physically learn that much content in just one year!? Dispelling the anxiety: At my school, everyone (i.e., 150 of us) did one Anticipated subject. Some schools even allow people to take 2 Anticipated subjects. Achieving a grade 7 in Anticipated is also very feasible. So don't worry, the workload is doable.

You can only choose SL subjects to Anticipate. Most subjects are great to Anticipate, but I would personally stay away from the more notorious Anticipated subjects. History is already infamously difficult as a two-year course. I personally wouldn't select it as an Anticipated subject. English A Literature or Lang Lit – a very small number of 7s for the two-year course, so I wouldn't bet on getting a 7 in Anticipated. Mathematics – university admissions tend to require at least two years of senior Mathematics. However, Mathematics is one of those courses that works well with Anticipated. Maths is more about practice and I think you can pick up maths skills quickly. Second language subjects are fantastic to Anticipate if you are already somewhat proficient in the language.

I would advise most people to Anticipate a Group 3 Humanities subject (apart from History, of course!):

Psychology – a lot of people at my school did this. It worked great for me, but Psychology is a lot of rote learning and material. It's not an easy ride by any means, but it is probably more manageable than History.

Business and Management – even more people at my school anticipated B&M. Many people have the impression that it's an 'easy' subject, but I can't say anything on the topic because I've never done it. In the end, all subjects take time and commitment. Choosing the right anticipated subject is about knowing your strengths and considering the costs and benefits for you personally.

Doing an Anticipated subject is a good way to minimize stress and sleep deprivation in your second year of IB, with the trade-off being a slightly greater workload during your first year. You experience a real IB exam before you do all your other exams in final year. I found that the familiarity with the exam procedure really helped with nerves and pre-exam anxiety.

6. Do the Basics Right

The purpose of this chapter is to provide some basic guidelines and daily basis advice you should follow to survive in the world of IB. The degree to which you follow the advice in this chapter depends on what type of student you are. If organization, motivation and promptness are second nature to you then you will find most of the information in this chapter somewhat obvious.

Attendance

Although some of your classmates may beg to differ, missing school does not make you a modern-day Ferris Bueller. You must ensure that you are attending class as often as you can. Most of your classes are very demanding, and even one or two days missed could mean a lot in terms of catching up with the material. No matter how useless you think a certain class is, I would still recommend you show up because it is good work ethic and it will keep you busy.

In the rare case that you miss class because of an illness or any other valid reason, make sure that you talk to your teacher and get the correct material that you may have missed. Those of you who skip class regularly will find that sympathy is hard to come by when you have a genuine reason for your tardiness. This is yet another reason to avoid unnecessarily skipping class.

Free Periods

The term 'free period' has varying interpretations from student to student and school to school. To some of you this may mean an hour of playing solitaire on your laptop, to others it may mean an opportunity to finish last night's homework. Similarly, some schools are more stringent than others. At my school, most teachers treated 'free periods' as a quiet one-hour study session where students were free to do work independently. I want you to make the most out of the time available. Whether you do work, socialize, or catch up on sleep – make sure that it is not time wasted and that you are doing something that will benefit your grades in the long run.

Some schools allow students to arrive later (if the free periods are in the morning) or to depart before school is over (if the free periods are in the afternoon). Find out if you can do the same, and decide whether you would benefit from this. On occasion, I would try to miss any free period at the end of the day and get home to catch up on some sleep. You need to work out whether this is possible, and feasible.

Understandably, some schools simply do not allow students to have 'free periods'. Many of you studying in the US will find that any period not devoted to the IB will be packed with an alternative high school curriculum. Some schools prefer to devote more time to extra-curricular activities, or keep students busy with extra classes. If this is the case, then great. If you are being kept busy and productive, then you are on the right track.

Note Taking

Personally, I was never that great at taking notes in class. My handwriting was poor, and I found it difficult to take in everything that was being discussed and simultaneously jot down effective notes. I figured that if I can engage in the conversation and understand what the teacher is trying to say, then I could write down more effective notes after class. Unfortunately, too often I would forget.

Effective note taking is not something that can be mastered in a few months, let alone a few weeks. It took me nearly two years of university lectures to finally be able to write and process information fast enough to take very helpful notes.

I find that this habit differs in difficulty across students. If handwriting is your biggest concern, try to bring a laptop. A more drastic alternative (and one that should only be used during the most important and difficult sessions) would be to bring a voice recorder and make notes afterwards. Of course, this involves a great deal of dedication and motivation, however I do remember certain HL Mathematics classes where a voice recorder proved to be a life-saver.

There are two key things to remember when taking notes. One is to make sure that everything you write down isn't already explained in detail in your textbook and/or previous notes. This is very inefficient and you are better off simply listening and letting the information seep into your memory. The second thing to keep in mind is to only write down notes that make sense. If you find yourself writing words that are unfamiliar to you, then you are wasting your time. You need to raise your hand and ask the question.

You may find yourself lucky enough to have a friend or two who take outstanding notes. Although getting great notes from a fellow peer is better than having nothing at all, I would still be cautious before resorting to this option. No matter how good the notes are, they will never be as valuable to you as something you wrote down yourself.

In recent years with the rising populatirty of Tumblr and Instagram, some students have begun to take great pride in their notes and photograph their hand-written works of art. They are called 'studyspo' or 'studygram's – and it is worth checking them out. It may inspire you to perhaps start taking clearer and better notes. Whether this will help you memorize the material better is an altogether different question.

7. Student-Teacher Relations

This chapter is not only important for your time in the IB program – but it is an essential skill to acquire if you want to be successful in life and get ahead. The skill I'm referring to here is, in the crudest sense, the skill of getting what you want from people in higher positions of power. You've probably already engaged in this in one form or other as a child manipulating your parents to get what you want, but as you get older the players in that game change, and your tactics adjust accordingly.

Now that being said, I would like to take a moment to remind you that being a teacher is one of the hardest and most underappreciated careers in the world. There is no glamor, and the pay isn't proportional to the amount of effort (most) teachers put in. Of all the people you will encounter in your short stay on this planet, your teachers are one of the few characters who genuinely want the best for you and care about your future and your well-being – and for that they deserve respect and gratitude. If you treat them well, you will get treated well in return.

Get used to it: teachers are your new best friends. Despite what teachers say, they do have favourite students and these lucky kids get preferential treatment (I was one of them). These students get this treatment as there is a greater level of trust and dialogue between them and the teacher, which makes the teacher more lenient. What does "lenient" entail, well...

1. Teachers will be more lenient when it comes to deadlines and will accept your work in late and still give feedback allowing you to submit better versions of your work at later dates (this can be useful as time allows you to spot your own mistakes).
2. The feedback teachers give you will be more detailed and comprehensive as they believe their

advice won't go to waste; hence, they don't mind the extra effort.

3. When time comes to grading both report cards and predicted grades the teachers will be optimistic. They believe that you are a good student and over time you will progress; hence if you are between grade boundaries you are likely to get marked up. Even better and more daring is the fact that you can discuss you grade. For example, if you know that it is important for you to get a 7 in physics (and you are getting high level 6s), you can discuss it with your teacher and ask them for that grade, justifying why you will be able to reach it. A few methods of justification would be as follow:

   a. Show them you planned revision, for example if you will be attending any summer courses or if you have bought anything that can help you improve at the subject. This proof should be tangible and significant.

   b. If you start the year with 5s in test and are ending on 7s, your teacher might be tempted to give you a 6; however you can show him or her that you actually have shown progress and you "believe" you deserve a 7.

4. You can have detailed and private conversations on matters such as homework, IAs, exams, tests and things that you don't understand in your subject. Remember all the information you receive is useful if used properly.

Don't forget it, teachers are humans too, they have their faults and they are usually very fun people. Get to know them and you will understand how they think, and ultimately how they grade. But even more than that, you will have a great time in class learning and interacting with these interesting people. I can say as a matter of fact that I liked all my teachers both as academics and as people, we got along very well and even joked around.

IB co-ordinator

Although your interactions with this faculty member may be limited, they hold the key to your IB diploma – you do not want to piss this person off. Everything from choosing subjects to submitting crucial coursework on time, they will oversee. Understandably IB coordinators will vary in experience from school to school, but do your best to get on good terms and make sure they know how serious you are about achieving your diploma.

Remember that it's in this person's best interest to make sure the entire class does well on their IB. It will reflect poorly on them if students fail to get their diploma. For that reason, if there is something you feel will increase the scores of the students, you should share your thoughts with the coordinator. For example, if you feel like you need new textbooks or you feel like you desperately need to change class, they are the person to go and see.

In the following section I will go over a few key faculty members and try to explain the importance of fostering a healthy relationship. I am aware that not every school will be lucky enough to have a designated person for each role, but nonetheless the advice will be applicable.

CAS Coordinator

See Chapter 43: Conquering CAS

The Principal

The idea here is pretty simple – don't mess up and get into disciplinary trouble. Although they don't have an impact on your IB grades directly, they do have the power to kick you out of school if you are a jackass, so just don't be one.

Extended Essay Supervisor

See Chapter 38: Excel at the Extended Essay [Part II]

Subject-Specific Teachers

Obviously, these factulty members are very important. From you IA work, to your predicted grades, to helping you revise for the subject – your daily teachers are instrumental to your IB success. You will see them almost every day, so you better make a great first impression. If you show them that you care about getting top marks, they will provide you with the necessary tools.

Will you click and get along with each one of them? No, probably not. Some will be more problematic than others, but learning the skill of getting past that is something that you will cherish for the rest of your life. You need to understand that part of the game here is just playing the part. Do what they want you to do and then it will be much easier to ask them to do you favours.

Make sure to pay close attention to the details of the assignments that your teacher gives (yes, the details). Basically, you need to know exactly what your teachers wants. It might even be worth asking students who have had your teacher before what they want and what they like. Asking questions is also crucial to gaining your teacher's respect – basically don't be invisible, and don't let shyness get in the way of your learning.

If the teacher wants you to have a laptop and TI-84, have a laptop and TI-84. If they say you need a silver Mickey-Mouse balloon, have that. Don't skimp on required class supplies, even if inconvenient or expensive. It will handicap you. Again, you want to do everything you can to satisfy the teacher's expectations.

As covered in the chapter on subject choices – there will inevitably be teachers who you deem 'not good enough' to be teaching their subject. This happens, it's part of life. But that doesn't mean you have an excuse to just give up. You will need to take that subject much more seriously and do lots of independent study (great preparation for university). This is where our advice on revision and internal assessments will come in handy.

Keep in mind that the internal assessment means just that – *internal*. This means your teacher will be the one to give it a grade. Ultimately, a sample will be sent off to the IBO to be 'moderated' if marks are too high or too low, but this won't matter much if you've created such friction with your teacher that your IA marks are horrible. Teacher bias during IA marking is something that does occur, but you should be doing your best to mitigate this.

If there are some serious issues that can't be resolved with a certain teacher, you should seek to find a solution by approaching your IB co-ordinator. The hierarchy for resolving problems should be as such: teacher, then head of department (if there is one), then IB coordinator, then principle, then parents. Most problems can be overcome with simple dialogue. Finally, be polite to your teachers / professors and subtly let them know you wish to succeed in their class. Don't be a suck up, but don't be rude or lazy either. Grading practices are never completely objective, despite what you might hear - or how hard teachers might try to make it so.

University Counsellor

Another extremely important individual – both for US and UK bound students. Plan a trip to their office sometime early in the first year – maybe even over the summer. Discuss your options and get as many resources as possible (they might have some great university application books in their office). The university counsellor should help you with all things application related, but you would also be wise to do some research on your own.

Grade Predictions

Your subject teachers (and EE/TOK for that matter) will be required to submit grade predictions for your university applications. Here is where student-teacher relationships are crucial. Predicted grades are a tricky obstacle for any IB student. Nine times out of ten, students will feel that they are being under-predicted. Many schools refuse to disclose the predictions to students because they anticipate a large angry group of kids mobbing them with protests after school hours. Nonetheless, predicted grades are the golden ticket when it comes to university offers. If your predicted grades are below the usual entry standards, the chances of you receiving an offer from a UK university are slim to none.

Here is my simple advice when it comes to maximizing your chances of getting the best predicted grades: negotiation. The matter of the fact is that teachers often look at things like homework grades, test results and class participation as an indicator of how well you will do in the final IB examinations. Although some of those things may play a small role, the truth is that the best predictors of your final results are: internal assessments (coursework that counts towards your final grade), how well you take IB examinations, how well you prepared in the few months before examinations, and a small element of random luck. Luck and exam revision aside, the other two components are fairly easy to analyse.

If your teachers insist on looking at test scores and random homework assignments as a way to judge your future success in the final exams, you need to persuade them that your high-scoring courseworks (which account for 20-40% of final subject grades in most subjects) and your ability to study past-paper questions and handle mock exams are both a far better indicator of how well you will do. I understand that this is easier said than done, but I do remember spending a good week or so visiting various teachers after-hours to convince them that despite my so-so homework grades or sometimes uninspired class participation, I will score highly on my diploma because I know what counts and I know how to play the IB system. Those of you who have read my IB help book will know exactly what I am talking about.

Letter of Recommendation

It is imperative that the person who you choose to write your reference for university applications is not only highly literate, but more importantly can fill the reference full of praise and admiration. Obviously, the person writing your reference should be closely related to the subject you intend to study at university. There are minor exceptions to this. For example, when I was applying to study economics, my economics teacher at school did not necessarily dislike me, however I did feel that they would not put all their efforts into writing a stand-out reference and perhaps it would not be as elegantly written. Instead, I sought the help of my geography teacher (who happened to hold a PhD from LSE, and had previously taught economics and business at a high school level). The teacher in question clearly saw a lot of potential in me, so I asked for help and got a wonderfully written reference in return. Whomever you seek for this task, make sure they are not going to write a generic reference but instead something personal and something that will make you stand out.

The real objective of student-teacher relations in the IB is: 'why do work when you can get others to do it for you?'; some people call it 'leverage'. Unfortunately, getting your teachers to help doesn't mean you can just laze at home and do nothing. You need to make life easy for them - make plans, make time to see them, organize everything, be ready when they ask you questions. If you keep up a disciplined image, they will be lots more likely to take you seriously. For IAs...they can only mark one draft, but go see them in their office and make them read over edited parts again and again. They want you to get a 7.

Yes, I understand that some teachers are quite unfriendly/unknowledgeable and so you don't want to see them. That's alright too. Just make sure you have everything under control and you haven't upset the wrong people.

8. Maximizing Productivity at School

If only I had an IB point for every time I heard someone mutter the words 'what, we had homework?' Keeping an agenda or a daily planner is a very simple solution to keeping track of what is due when. Make a habit of writing down important dates as soon as you hear about them. The IB does a pretty good job at reminding students about the big deadlines (Extended Essay, External Assesment, CAS portfolio) however any internal deadlines you may have are your responsibility to note.

There's no reason to go old-school when it comes to organisation. With the rise in popularity of iPhones, and personal laptops, it has become much easier for you to electronically set reminders. These items are also more likely to be consulted, and less likely to be lost than a simple paperback agenda.

Health

This is NOT a self-help book and nor do I ever intend to offer life advice to anyone. However, I do think it is worthwhile at least briefly mentioning the importance of things like eating right and exercising.

Research has shown time and time again that physical activity is crucial in maintaining mental well-being. IB students often report negative moods, irritability, and other stress-related problems. All of this can lead to more complicated emotional concerns. Exercise is a good combatant in your fight to a healthy physical and mental well-being.

Even just 20 minutes of exercise can lead to higher energy levels. You will find it easier to sit down and concentrate on your studies and may even feel more motivated. Also, you can easily combine exercise with socialising. Having someone to talk to while jogging or at the gym can be a great stress-reliever – just make sure the conversation steers clear of IB-related matters.

Just as important as regular exercise is keeping an eye on what you are eating. If you ever felt exhausted despite not really doing anything, or get easily distracted when you should be working, this could be down to your choice or lack of foods.

Although our brain is only about 2% of our total body mass, it consumes roughly 20% of the energy you take in. when we concentrate the brain uses up to 200 kilocalories per hour – or 10% of your daily food intake. So next time you skip breakfast, or have a very late lunch keep in mind that your brain needs a steady supply of nutrients – many of which come from food.

For those more curious about how they can maximize brain function and energy levels with their diet, I strongly suggest you consider the 'ketogenic diet'. Many studies have reported that eating a diet high in fats and protein and low in carbohydrates (under 20g per day) results in 'brain clarity' and many individuals feel less lazy and more motivated – crucial attributes for academic success. I learned about ketosis and the ketogenic diet only when at university, however it has helped me greatly since then.

Homework

When it comes to homework, it is very difficult to prescribe specific advice because people have different preferences that work best for them. Personally, I found that doing homework in the late evening or at night was the most effective. This worked for me as there were little distractions and there was a sense of urgency which kept me motivated.

Besides timing, you also need to consider working effectively for concentrated amounts of times with no breaks. Ideally, working for 20 minutes non-stop with no outside interference and then rewarding yourself with a small break seems to be among the ideal strategies. Some of you may find that you work best with music in the background, or that your multitasking skills are so good that you can afford to flip your computer tabs from Facebook to iTunes to your lab report every few minutes. It's difficult to change this habit, and unless it is seriously damaging the quality of your work, I would not worry too much about it.

One tip that I found to work very nicely when doing homework was to save my favourite material for last. Getting all the difficult and less-favourable work out of the way early will not only lessen the chances of simply not doing it, but you will also have something to look forward to. Of course, one should be careful not to rush through the harder material just for the sake of 'getting it out the way' before moving onto the more enjoyable material.

Be heard

No matter how timid and shy you may be, there will be days when you simply need to make a formal comment or complaint about something that concerns you. In order to do this you need to build a constructive relationship with your IB Coordinator and any other influential teachers. This is much easier said than done.

Learn how to talk to authoritative figures. If you book a meeting with your IB Coordinator, then do not show up unprepared. If you show them that you care, they will care too. The same goes for most teachers. If you show an interest and a longing for help (perhaps by asking for a contact email or number to reach them at after-school hours) then they are more than likely to respond positively.

Helpful Apps and Software

Smartib iOS/Android app – this is the app that I spent the last two years developing. It's a social media platform and community forum app designed specifically for students undergoing the IB Diploma program. The app allows students to create a profile and connect with other IB students all over the world via a well-organised forum where they can ask and answer questions. At this time, the app is still in its growing phase, but I imagine we will have the majority of IB students using it by the end of the 2017.

Evernote – excellent note taking software, and free. Learn to use the software beforehand, there are lots of features that you may find come in handy.

Todoist – free and great to-do list app. Use it if you don't have a day planner/agenda. It also links up with google calendar/default Mac calendar.

OneNote – the following advice is paraphrased from one of my former students and is incredibly helpful. I strongly recommend you follow it for your note-taking if you use a laptop:

1. Create a Notebook for one of your subjects (the one with the smallest number of characters)
2. Create a "section group" called term 1 (or whatever measurement you use)
3. Create a "section" along the top called "week"

Then set it up like this

<u>Class work</u>

This is for stuff you do in class that you won't really need to look over when revising. Sometimes I just work in here for a class then take key elements out and put it into keynotes. But If I know what we are doing is just notes (like core concepts in maths or an English slideshow)

<u>Keynotes</u>

This is the stuff that you need from the class. The things that you would give a friend if they missed a class. Make sure that you type keywords, topics, connections (if you are doing a poem that mentions another poem if you put the name of the other poem). This is so that you can search for them later (maybe have a table that you put off to the side)

<u>Assessment</u>

This one is for longer projects like oral notes or things you do for more than one class
Make sure you either title them well or remember where they are

<u>Setting up all the classes quickly</u>

So this is where it gets a bit confusing. So you now have to find where your OneNote files are saved (default is "C:\Users[your name]\Documents\OneNote Notebooks". If not, then: Right click on one of your Notebooks, go to properties, click "change location", then open the same position in file explorer (or equivalent)

You should have a folder for whatever subject you choose in the "set up" . Open it and then open "term 1". Copy the file in there called "week"* Paste it And rename it week 2. Repeat for each week in the term.

After you have a file for each week "week 1" to "week 9" (or how many weeks you have in a term) Then go back to "term 1" Copy and paste it 3 times and rename it, "term 2" to "term 4". Then go back to the folder with your subject in. Copy and paste it for each subject. Rename them respectively. Put all of these into a folder called year 11 (or equivalent). Copy and paste this folder and rename it year 12. If you choose to implement any of the subject-specific things, add them at this stage.

Subject-Specific OneNote advice:

Psychology

Have a weekly subgroup for writing essays and study summaries (like Assessment but specifically for essays/studies). Maybe break this down into the levels of analysis (bio, cog, social cultural and your 2 options). Remember to use keywords and use the question exactly from the syllabus (so you can find it more easily). If you are smart with what studies you use, you can use some for many different questions.

English Literature

Similar to Psych, keep essays apart. Have a dedicated place for feedback from teachers (probably good for all subjects in fact) write notes for all your meeting

Maths Studies

You can do notes in OneNote by pressing "alt+ =" (the alt key and the equals key). There are lots of shortcuts within in this. If you have a touch screen/stylus it can be good write draw them straight into OneNote (there is an ink feature)

Language Ab

Have a place for words
Try to have the English (first language), your language, Example, any exceptions Useful phrases followings similar structures as the words. As of the other subject, I haven't done them so pick the elements that relate to the parts (I know that might be hard) tricks

This advice is written for OneNote 2016, so some of these may not work on other versions. You can write maths in notation by pressing "alt+ =" (the alt key and the equals key). You can use it like a calculator such as " $3^\wedge4+(3/2)=$" Then put a space afterwards and it should solve it if it doesn't work make sure there are no letters or non-mathematical things touching the equation.

You can write with a pen if you have a touch screen. It Auto Saves but be careful to backup. If you want to really focus, try this View-> Always Pin on Top.

A OneNote page is infinitely large (this is both an advantage and a massive disadvantage). You can turn on grids which help's (me) organise things on a page. You can make lots of different boxes which makes Selection (see Cntrl+A) and comparing things easier.

9. The Importance of IA

Internal Assessment (IA) is the easiest, most effective and fastest way to get top marks in almost all your subjects. You would have to be extremely ignorant to ignore that fact. Try doing some simple math. If we say that, on average, IA takes up roughly 25% of your grade for each subject then that means it takes up ¼ of the maximum grade 7 per subject – nearly two entire points. Now, this may not seem like much, but when you consider that you have 6 subjects plus the 3 bonus points from TOK/EE – this adds up to 15 points towards your IB diploma. Simply put: from maxing out on your Internal Assessment and EE/TOK you can get 15 marks even before you step into the examination room.

That's the beauty of it. You have no idea what a comforting feeling it is walking into the exam room knowing you already have 12 – 15 points in the bag. One must try to remain realistic. No matter how much you have studied, no matter how many past papers you have done, and no matter how well you have grasped the material, what happens on the exam day will to a certain extent be outside of your control. What if you break an arm, get a stomach ache or become ill during the exam? What if all three happen? What if your co-coordinator makes a mistake and forgets to give you a periodic table for your HL Chemistry exam (as has happened)? What if you just "go blank" when you open your exam and forget all that you have crammed the night before?

I have seen some of the best IB candidates underperform on exam day simply because of bad luck and misfortune. Another likely scenario is that you are simply not an exam person. I am usually very comfortable with the material, spend plenty of time studying, and usually can answer most questions when asked verbally in a non-exam situation. However, when the clock is ticking and the pressure is on, I tend to only perform at about 80% of my potential. I am not an "exam person". In fact, I hate examinations because so many factors are outside of your control. There are too many ways in which one can make careless mistakes and mess up.

As I was trying to point out, IA makes up roughly 25% of your grade for each subject. In subjects such as English it amounts to nearly 30% of the grade. So even before you sit your English exam, you are nearly 1/3rd done. This means that if you have done amazingly well on your IA, you already have 2 or 3 marks secured towards your English grade. It is a very comforting feeling to know that no matter how poorly you perform on your exam, you are almost definitely in the 4 to 7 range – in other words you are comfortably going to pass. This may not mean much to the more ambitious candidates reading this manual. If you are amongst the IB candidates who worry about failing the IB diploma, then this IA stuff can save you.

Now some of you may still need further convincing that Internal Assessment is extremely important. The words 'lab report', 'economic commentary' and 'World Literature paper' are so often used in the same breath as the word 'homework' that students forget to realise the importance of IA. The points add up, and before you know it, it might be too late to go back and capitalize on your IA marks.

Let's think about this logically. The assessment is usually given a week or even a few weeks in advance. For bigger assignments, such as the Extended Essay you have substantially more time to prepare. You are given weeks to complete something that will account for a generous fraction of your final grade. Now contrast this with the final examinations, which will usually take up the remaining 60% - 75% of your final grade. The exam duration per subject is rarely more than 6 or 7 hours. Those few hours will decide what you will get for the remaining portion of your grade. Would it not make sense then to work relentlessly on maximizing your mark for the IA simply because you are given so much more time and space? The final examination goes by in a blink of an eye whereas you are given an abundance of time to work on your IA. Once you realise this, you will make sure your IAs are as flawless as possible.

You are given weeks, if not months, to decide nearly a fourth of your grade, and then you are given two or three hours to decide the remaining three-fourths. It would be foolish to put in less effort for the IA then the actual examinations. They are practically handing you these marks. No matter how poorly you know the material, or how poorly you perform on examinations, nearly anyone can ace their Internal Assessment – especially given the advice provided further in this guide.

So, if you are one of those people who tend to underperform in examinations and simply can't bother studying, you absolutely need to take full advantage of the IA. It baffles me as to why so many students fail to see this loophole. Even the top IB candidates often focus so much on learning the material and doing well in the actual exams that they lose track of the fact that IA also counts towards the final grade.

With regards to the order of importance for IB-related daily matter, I would suggest the following rank: 1) Internal Assessment, 2) revision for tests, 3) homework. This means that if you have a lab report due in tomorrow and a test as well, you need to finish and polish the lab before you even start thinking about revising for the test. Tests will come and go, but you will have few opportunities to redo your Internal Assessments.

All the labs, coursework, portfolios and papers that make up your IA are of far greater importance than any test or homework assignment that you must do. Yes, your trimester grade may suffer. Yes, the teacher may get on your back for not doing the homework. Nonetheless, you need to keep a voice in the back of your head telling you that "at the end of the day, small tests and homework won't give me my 7's, the IB assessment will." Word of caution: if you have teachers who heavily rely on homework and tests as predicted grade markers, you will need to reconsider this advice.

Also, many students use IAs as an excuse to stop doing homework. This is a bad idea because homework is not 'skipped'. It only piles up and comes back to haunt you. We all know that there are two categories of homework...the necessary kind and the unnecessary kind. For example, necessary homework would be a Chemistry worksheet on Organic structures that is marked by your teacher as an assignment. Unnecessary homework would be a stack of 500 equation-balancing problems (you can do this slowly, especially if your teacher isn't collecting it).

The beauty behind Internal Assessment is that literally anyone, of any academic ability, can get top marks. This is great news for those of you who do not plan on studying much for the exams, or who are terrified of test-taking. All you need to do is spend an incredible amount of time constantly improving and upgrading your assignment. I have seen some pretty daft IB students ace their assignments simply because they spent day and night perfecting them. Although they may have not been academically gifted, at least they realised the potential impact that IA could have on their grades – and in that sense, they are geniuses.

It doesn't matter whether you are "smart". You simply need to be ruthless when it comes to completing your IA assignments. Follow the guidelines that I provide in this book for each subject on how to maximize your IA. If you do that, then regardless of how good or bad you think you are at a certain subject, you will be able to get a "handicap" of +2 on your final grade before you sit the exam.

You need to become the King (or Queen) of IA in your class. All the other students will be in awe as you get 19/20 back for your Math IA or a near full marks for your Economics portfolio. They may say you are wasting your time aiming for the perfect IA assessment, but when you get your final grades back you will be laughing at them. You need to strive to have the best coursework possible.

I remember a few months before final examinations some teachers would announce whose work was getting sent off to be moderated. Now, I don't know how the system works inside out, but I have a feeling that for IA the IBO demands that a good distribution of student work is sent off. In other words: the top assignments, the average assignments and the assignments at the lower end of the grading scale. I would look around the class to see who else was having their work sent off, and immediately I could tell that my work was part of the "top assignments" (our teacher never told us whose work got selected). This took a lot of stress off the final examinations. It is incredible feeling when you are revising to know that you are 25% closer to getting your 7s.

Getting top marks in your IA is not an easy task. Then again, neither is getting 7's in your examinations. The key difference is that whereas with the exams you are given a few hours to show your worth, the IA timeline is much more generous. You will need to work late nights, weekends, and holidays to get top marks for your IA. In fact, you would probably work just as hard (if not harder) a few weeks prior to your exams, so I don't see why this would be such a daunting task.

You need to develop a habit of wanting to strive for perfection in all your externally moderated IAs. Treat this as being just as important as the actual exam, or even more so. I want you to start feeling extremely disappointed if you are getting back labs/commentaries/portfolios that are below a grade 6. Not only should you be getting 7's, you should be getting high 7's. Keep in mind that what your teacher thinks you deserve is not the final grade. It will be moderated and probably hiked up or down a few notches. You should therefore make sure to leave a little room for change when you are told your predications.

Given the fact that you reading this book, I think I can safely assume that you are not the naturally gifted IB diploma student who is predicted to get a 45. You may struggle getting 6's or even 5's on your school tests. At the same time, you may be a student who is borderline failing the diploma program and is anticipating the worst when the final examinations come around. In either case, this advice about IA is of equal importance. IA can turn a failing IB diploma grade of 15 to a 30. Or a 30 to a 45. The important thing is that you take this advice and follow it through.

I firmly believe that if a student maxes out on his/her IA, then it is nearly impossible to fail the IB diploma. You will get somewhere around 15 marks for your assignments alone (given that you get all 3 bonus marks), which leaves just about 10 more marks from your actual examination. I have yet to meet a person that cannot scrape 10 marks on their actual examinations. If you maximize your IA marks, then you are entering a stress-free world of examinations. Instead of deciding where you will be on a scale of 0 to 45, you now can estimate your final grade on a scale of 15 to 45.

I know I am getting repetitive but you need to drill this into your head. You need to strive for perfection on your Internal Assessment. Do that and you are one step, one giant leap, closer to getting what you want from your IB diploma. Don't be ignorant, realise the power of IA marks and the effect that they can have on your final grade. You don't know how much you will hate yourself when you find out that the reason you missed out on getting your dream grade of 45 was due to a poorly done IA that dragged you down to a 44 overall. Or how about finding out that the only reason you failed IB was because you "forgot" to hand in an Economics commentary and this dragged you down below 24 marks. Be smart: milk the IA for all that it is worth.

It's a miracle that a notoriously "rigorous" program such as the IB diploma program would have nearly 25% of the final score decided on a non-exam basis. You are lucky that final grades aren't based entirely on your ability to perform well in exams as is the case in many other high school programs worldwide. This provides a great opportunity to those of you who are hard-working and intelligent, yet lack that cutting edge when it comes to examinations. Take full advantage of this – it won't be long before the IB starts to diminish the importance of Internal Assessment (they already have over the last decade) and add greater value to the actual examinations.

Students stress about final exams, but in this case you'll have got a whole bunch of grades before you even get to them. This has an extraordinary implication for you. Imagine an exam system in which they ask you whatever you want to study, let you decide how to study and even let you write some of the questions. This is basically the IB system: between 20% and 40% of your grades you can get from work that you can write, check, triple-check, get friends and families to advise you, change work, mark yourself, and work out certainly what mark the examiner will give.

IAs are the only aspect of IB that you have real 'control' over. You get to write your own questions and come up with your own answers. As mentioned, most IAs also make up at least 20% of your final grade and do make the difference between 6s and 7s. For example, if you got a low 5 on your Maths IA, you'd need to get 95+% on the final exam to get a 7; if you got a 7 already, you can make do with about 80%. That 15%, as we all know, is a huge difference. Don't treat IAs like projects in middle school. They are imperative and, as I believe, designed to help you gain marks before the final exams.

With regards to time management, I'm sure that nobody wants to hand in a crap IA. It's just that we are sometimes forced to that point by outside pressures, i.e. lack of time. What many students need to understand is that time is 'created', not 'found'. Nature does not give you any time, you need to squeeze it out by yourself. Confucius probably said something about time being like 'water in a sponge'. Unfortunately, time in the IB world is more like 'maple syrup in a sponge', and is hard to eke out. It is nevertheless possible to maintain high standards on your IAs.

General IA Advice

1) You need to choose the right question. This is where many candidates fail, as they are over-ambitious and bite off more than they can chew. Choose a question that you're interested in, but which also pertains to the course. Yes, IB is about learning, but also about passing. Also, get advice on your question ASAP. Even when the teacher has just announced the IA. Brainstorm as fast as possible, and ask for a quality check on your ideas. This saves you lots of time in the long run.

2) 'Why do work when you can get others to do it for you?' is an age-old technique; some people call it 'leverage'. Unfortunately, getting your teachers to help doesn't mean you can just laze at home and do nothing. You need to make life easy for them - make plans, make time to see them, organise everything, be ready when they ask you questions. If you keep up a disciplined image, they will be lots more likely to take you seriously. For IAs...they can only mark one draft, but go see them in their office and make them read over edited parts again and again. They want you to get a 7.

3) Yes, I understand that some teachers are quite unfriendly/unknowledgeable and so you don't want to see them. That's alright too. You just need to replicate the 'teacher' process at home. You need to set goals for yourself. Don't say 'I need to get this done before July because it is the deadline'. You should tell yourself, "The first draft is due to myself/IB gods on 15 June." Get a friend to help you with accountability if needed - make sure to return the favour.

4) Squeezing out time is a special art. You need to look at your current life and do a 'time budget'. What are you

spending time on? What can you cut out? It's like calorie counting but with minutes.

I know these measures sound quite 'hardcore' but...you will thank yourself when the final exams arrive and you know that you don't have to get an impossible score in order to reach your goal. This can actually give you a major confidence boost when it matters the most. Spread out your suffering. Piling up IAs are like cars. When you have an accident on the highway, they tend to pile up.

When faced with a developing or fully-developed pile, the first thing you need to do is be honest with yourself. Take a survey of the situation and write down all that you must do. Then do these by priority. Many students confuse 'priority' with 'preference'. Yes, doing your History IA is more fun than making graphs for your Math IA. But if your Math IA is due next week and the History IA is due next month, don't even think about doing History first. If you're having too much fun with a pileup on your plate, chances are...you're not prioritising.

You can also try a 'war of attrition' against your work, but this is more of a pre-emptive measure. Basically, do a bit of work at every available opportunity. Social lives are important but...if you need that extra 20 minutes, man up, skip recess, and do your chemistry assignment. That 20 minutes can then be saved at home for EE writing purposes. Basically every second counts.

With regards to sleep, you don't need to stay up till 3am or pull an all-nighter. Most people go to school from 8am to 3pm or similar hours. What are you doing from 4pm to 10pm? That's a full 6 hours for you to get some stuff done. You have months to do your IAs. The rest of your time can be used for study, recreation, and much-needed sleep. You don't feel it, especially if you're hopped up on caffeine, but your work quality is going to be lower after a whole day of school and not sleeping.

One final pro-tip: get your hands on the subject reports. These are reports where the examiners explain what exactly was good or bad in last year's IAs (and exams) and give a whole section of advice to teachers and students on how to do better. Your teacher should have them, and you should seek these out.

10. Managing Stress

There is no hiding from the fact that the IB Diploma program can be very stressful. There will be certain weeks or days where you will feel like you are juggling six plates with the weight of the academic world on your shoulders and a ball and chain with the words 'EE' and TOK' around your legs. Nonetheless, I will now introduce a few tips to help you deal with the strain and anxiety.

Nutrition

Ah, food. Food is good. So, eat something. Don't stuff your face with crap all the time. Be reasonably healthy and save all the beautiful fried chicken for the weekend. Eating properly has a great effect on your energy levels. Don't starve yourself either. Working on an empty rumbling stomach is like listening to a baby cry. They can both be stopped with some warm milk and cookies.

The stereotype of the IB student as someone surviving on caffeine, Pot Noodles, and energy drinks is, in many cases, not a complete exaggeration. If you are up late at night busy working then you are more likely to consume foods and drinks that require little time to prepare and give a good energy boost. Although I have already reminded you about the benefits of eating right during your two years in the IB program, the exam period itself will pose its own challenges. Even if you are franticly revising all day and all night, try to still get your three meals a day and eat plenty of vitamin rich foods.

I found myself chewing a lot of gum during the late nights and the revision stages. Personally, I found that this helped me focus more and kept me awake. Those of you that smoke will probably find that you are smoking a lot more than normal. If you are a big coffee fan, then be careful not to overdo it.

Sleep

I'll be first to admit that the amount of sleep you will get during the two year IB program will probably be less than any other two year period of your life. On any given day, I could spot several of my fellow students drifting off during class, or having serious bags under their eyes from the lack of sleep.

Making sure that you get enough sleep is once again due to good time management skills. I found that I would come home from school too tired to be productive so I would make it a habit to get a couple hours sleep in the evening. Usually this would just be on the couch, but it was nonetheless enough for me to get up and feel reenergized. Studies have shown that even a 15 minute nap can be enough to make you feel revitalized.

You need to find out when you are at your most productive state. I slowly discovered throughout highschool that I worked best at night or at least the very late evening. Going to bed at 2 am was not uncommon during school nights, but this was fine for me because I would make up the hours by napping once I came home. Although it was hard to adjust to such a schedule I eventually made it routine. I enjoyed working at night because there was an added element of urgency and there was little room to procrastinate. Working under pressure is not for everyone, so you need to figure out what works best for you.

As an IB student you also need to learn to get sleep wherever and whenever you can. My bus ride to school took around an hour. I made sure that unless I had a test to study for or an assignment to complete I would try to sleep for most of that hour. Other classmates of mine would politely ask to nap during 'free periods' and sometimes this was permitted by the teacher. Those who pulled all-nighters would even try to nap during lunchtime after having something to eat.

Sleep is essential to being productive and motivated. A lack of sleep can result in careless errors in assignments and missing essential information in class. For the 16-18 year old age group, the recommended amount of sleep is usually quoted as 6-8 hours. If you are getting less than 5 hours on a regular basis then there might be cause for alarm. Remember that although this is only a two-year program, you could potentially be doing more long-term damage to your health by missing out on sleep.

Second-hand Stress

It is often said that being surrounded by negative people can be contagious. The same is true for stress. If you surround yourself with students that constantly complain about the workload and the pressure then you are more likely to succumb to their state. Make sure you have plenty of people to talk to that are on top of their work – this will also incentivize you to work harder and be more efficient.

Although you may think that by surrounding yourself with students who are behind on their work and always worrying will somehow make you feel better about your own situation, this is usually not the case. These people will make you worry more. You need to avoid this second-hand stress at all costs.

The Goal

Also, motivate yourself towards your goals. If you find no interest in working, the fact is you will not work. Just think about how good you'll feel once the exams are done.

Every crappy score you're getting right now is giving you a better chance at acing your finals. It means you've made lots of mistakes that you're never going to make again, because now you can learn from them. Don't let them get you down - focus on the feedback rather than the grade, and take it as a guide of how you can do better. If you're getting 6s now, there's room to improve. Doing past papers will make a huge difference.

Make time for yourself to just chill out, sleep, and be with friends. My friends and I tried to hang out regularly during senior year, even though it meant just sitting together in a library, each doing our own work. Give yourself a 5 minute break every 30 minutes. Walk around, stretch, do some push-ups. Exercise has been scientifically proven to be healthy. So you should do it. Preferably everyday if you can. It's a great way to release stress and make you feel good.

Stress at school is mainly caused by lack of organisation. So sorting that out could half or even eliminate your 'I want to rip the hair out of my head' feeling. Invest in a folder if you write notes with a note book and use folder separators to make things easier. This makes losing notes a lot less likely because they are in a named folder.

If you're feeling that things are getting to you, just step back for a little bit and think. You don't need to be getting overly stressed because that hinders your work and can result in tears, this isn't helpful to your development because it lowers your confidence. Try drinking some water, taking a short break from revision or going for a walk. Clear your mind.

(contributed article)

These are some brief thoughts about how to manage stress throughout the IB exam period and in general. I welcome anyone and everyone to share the techniques they use to manage stress.

Firstly, if you want to effectively reduce the amount of stress you feel with your workload, managing your time properly will help cut down on the level of stress you feel when working.

I'm not going to put any of these techniques in order because some people prefer different things. I should also mention that these techniques will only work if you actually use them. Don't just read them, ignore them, then come back after the exams and exclaim that your hair is turning grey because of stress.

It seems like when students think of studying they think of it as an extremely painful process which requires a lot of stress in order to be useful. 'You need to live in the library to get good results', 'studying is just student and dying put together' that sort of thing. None of that is true. You don't need to strain yourself while working in order to do well. You learn much better when you're relaxed.

Meditation

This is a great way to relax. I'd link you to a bunch of scientific studies about it but it's much better for you to try it and experience its usefulness first hand.

How do you get started?

Sit down (or lie down if you have back problems), and spend 5 to 10 minutes just focusing on your breathing. Don't try to alter your breath patterns. You'll probably find that it's quite difficult to just focus on your breath because thoughts will pop into your head but that's normal. Just gently return your focus to your breath. I'd recommend meditating at the start of the day then again at the end of the day if you want to.

Schedule time off

Don't cram your schedule with work and actually let yourself have a prolonged break. If you feel up to it, schedule a whole day off every week and do whatever you want absolutely guilt free. It will help you approach the next week with a bit more energy and you won't be a continuous battle with your work if you completely separate yourself from it for a while.

Have regular breaks

While trying to complete a huge task, it can be easy to lose track of where the time is going. Then you end up working for months without having a break. This can make you feel extremely frustrated when you're not making progress on something. However, you should wait until you feel like it. The point is to work with as little stress as possible. I'd recommend breaks as frequent as one every 25 to 30 minutes.

Plan your work

If you don't have any clear idea about what you're trying to accomplish then you'll always be an uphill battle. Take some time to make a detailed plan about what you want to do and when.

Also, assume you've underestimated the amount of time you'll need to complete something. If you've set aside 2 hours to think about an essay or make notes on a topic, give yourself 3 or 4. It'll stop you getting stressed about not being on schedule (that wasn't realistic in the first place) and give you spare time at the end of the day.

Clean yourself

Ok, admittedly that sounds like a dumb statement to make. But I have a point. I promise. There's very little point in being in an environment that either makes you feel like you're boiling or freezing or generally uncomfortable. So if your room feels stuffy, open your window a bit (and the curtains. I don't know why some people enjoy darkness so much. It makes no sense to me).

Groom yourself in the morning instead of groggily getting out of your bed and working away in pyjamas. Be comfortable but shower or something. If not for yourself, do it for everyone that'll come into your presence that day. You'll hopefully feel a bit more energized before you start your day.

Manage expectations

It's important to manage the expectations you have of yourself and the expectations other people have of you. We're often extremely self critical because we either just want the best for ourselves or there are visible pressures from other people. This isn't an admirable trait. Yes, we should try to find ways to improve our work but not at the expense of harmful negative talk and self-hatred. It isn't useful and won't help you progress at all.

If you don't complete all the tasks you wanted to complete that day, check if you've been too unrealistic, make the appropriate changes then forgive yourself. It won't change much in the long run especially if you've made changes which could improve how the next day goes.

If you find yourself talking negatively, ask whether you'd talk to a close friend the same way. If you wouldn't, you're probably being too harsh. Trust me; you do not deserve the negative self-talk you might put yourself through.

Have fun with friends

It might be odd to be reminded to talk to your friends but you should. You don't need to be in complete seclusion in order to be efficient. You can study alone but you don't need to be alone for the whole week. And enjoy time with them without feeling guilty! If you always feel guilty, you won't enjoy the company or get any work done. You'll just be in a weird purgatory that doesn't let you do anything.

11. Procrastination in the IB

(contributed article)

So, you now know how to maximize productivity and you're thinking that planning and getting on top of all your work seems like a pretty swell idea, but you have one major problem left: procrastination. It is one thing to plan and be organised, but it is another thing to follow that plan and get things done because they aren't going to get done by themselves.

Here are 5 easy steps to beat procrastination:

1. **Just 5 minutes** – start the task just for 5 minutes. Just do 5 minutes. Chances are, you'll be able to start, if not try any of the following.

2. **Break it down** – putting on your planner "Do EE" is a large and unreasonable task. Break it down into smaller chunks and work with one chunk at a time; e.g. gather research for EE. And then just do that (and tick it off). Each day, do a little more until it gets going. If the task is too hard for you, see what you can do first, then seek help after.

3. **Get away from your laptop/phone/internet** – put it in a different room, or turn it off. Honestly, I know how distracting Facebook is when you are in the mood to procrastinate. You'll find you will get going as soon as you can't get to it. If you need your laptop, use an app like Self Control to block your "procrastination sites".

4. **Plan a reward** – "After I do this, I can do whatever I want for the rest of the evening." Or, promise yourself that if you do everything you planned to during the week, you can take the weekend off – now that's a good deal!

5. **Keep busy** – don't leave yourself a ridiculous amount of time to do minuscule homework tasks that you'll put off anyway. Get involved! Go and play sport, hang out with friends, volunteer, then see

how well you work afterwards. Don't give yourself the time to procrastinate.

Procrastination is horrible. I hate it loads and I have a half decent way of sorting it out. Just know that you cannot get rid of it completely otherwise you'll probably end up not enjoying life. No one can seize every single opportunity they must work. It's just not realistic.

The reason why procrastination happens is because there are two parts of your brain. One part sees the short-term benefit of everything, like going on Facebook or staring into the sky. This part is much bigger than the part that sees the long-term benefit of working now. Plus, the long-term benefit part (the determined one) gets tired quickly. Ok, now imagine yourself as two people: 'present' you, and 'future' you.

What you need to remember is that it isn't now that you will be feeling the consequences of your procrastination, it will be future you. You need to look to future you and think that you want to have less work so you'll do it now. Procrastination isn't because you're lazy, it's because you're weak in the sight of distractions (that sounds mean but everyone gets distracted for the reason I stated above). Some overall advice:
- Keep your work neat.
    o You don't want to be revising and realise that you cannot read half of anything that you've written. Some care will go a long way.
    o You don't need to write full sentences when making notes, just something that can remind you what was taking place in class.
- Try organising your work daily.
    o This further reduces the chances of losing sheets and notes, hole punch it and keep it safe. You'd be surprised how much they can help .

- Lessen the distractions!
- Disable Facebook or move the Facebook app from the homepage of your phone.
- Mute your computer so you aren't hearing all sorts of notifications. Same goes for putting your phone off. Not on silent or vibrate – OFF.
- Clear the cookies from your computer so you must enter your password in every time you want to log into something. This makes logging into stuff an added effort so you're more inclined to just not bother and start your work. This process is automated if you use 'incognito mode' on your browser.
- Give yourself motivation
- Put pictures up of what you want to achieve (e.g. a 45 point diploma?)
- Plan a little treat you can have only if you've completed a certain amount of work, not if you've done something for a specific time. It's too easy to say 'I've read for half an hour, time to chill'.

Also, there is such a thing as 'helpful' procrastination. So when you feel lazy instead of refreshing the Facebook homepage, read an article from the news or a page from a book relating to your subjects. Or read a few more chapters from this book! In addition, don't mistake procrastination for having a break, breaks are good. They keep your sanity intact.

There is fundamental cognitive difference between procrastinators and normal people. Everyone gets overwhelmed by work sometimes. Even the busiest or most efficient people might feel overwhelmed when there's too much work and not enough time. But the procrastinator is different. The procrastinator might have plenty of time, however he puts off work until there isn't enough time and then feels scared, stressed and overwhelmed. This means the procrastinator makes his own life much worse – does that sound like anyone you know?

This sort of behaviour has a massive effect on our IB scores, both in exams and especially because of coursework. By putting things off and avoiding work we leave ourselves no time to work well. There's no time to complete tasks to our satisfaction and we end up with worse scores and worse universities than we could have reached.

So why do we keep procrastinating? When we keep making poor decisions which are illogical, the reason is almost always an emotional one. The three most common causes of chronic procrastination are fear, anxiety and shame. This could be fear that the work won't be good enough, that it won't score high enough, that peers will be better etc. Whatever the reason it is emotional and causes real problems. Fortunately, the problem tells us the solution.

Let's say you have a big project to do – maybe an Extended Essay, maybe revision for the IB exams. Whatever it is, you might find yourself procrastinating. If you're honest with yourself this is probably because you're worried that it won't be good enough. This is because the procrastinator only sees giant goals – so he sees 'The IB' as one goal, or Extended Essay as a goal. Of course these are impossibly big goals to take action on. But the non-procrastinator sees things differently. Non-procrastinators realise big goals are just groups of small tasks. While doing the EE might seem impossible, googling the markscheme, emailing your teacher for guidance and looking at the textbook are all easy tasks. And this is the secret: seemingly impossible tasks are just made of lots of very possible smaller tasks!

To change from a procrastination mindset to a non-procrastination one is not really that hard. The next time you start to feel nervous about a task grab a piece of paper and start to list all the things necessary to complete that task. Maybe to do an essay you would have to: do background research, find appropriate books, make a mind map, make a plan, write, edit and submit. Now focus on the first thing: for example, the research. What small tasks does the first thing include? Google the question, look at Wikipedia articles, look at the textbook. Now do that first small task, like checking the Wikipedia article on a certain topic.

That's it! You're working! Keep doing that over and over again and the essay will finish itself. It is possible to rewire your procrastinator brain. Now that you know how, test it out. Even at this moment you have things to do...yep! You just thought of one right? Probably one you really don't want to do. So grab some paper right now, I'll wait... Good! Now write the task name at the top and just start listing all things you have to do in that task. Ok, now write all the subtasks. If it looks too hard, just keep doing this. When you think you can do the first task, get going! And good luck!

12. IB Friendships

Friends are here to help you get through the IB and vice versa; it is therefore crucial that you surround yourself with the correct people. Throughout our 2 years of IB if it were not for certain friends we would not have been able to get the grades that we got. They reviewed our work, corrected mistakes they saw, helped us learn and explained things that we didn't understand. But most importantly, as cheesy as this may sound, your good friends will always be there for you.

I remember after the mock exams when a good friend of mine got a whopping 28% on his HL Math Paper 1. He was feeling horrible. I mean he had always been a great student: 7s in math during the MYP were no problem. But as you may know, HL Math is a totally different kind of beast. So, being one of his best friends, I really had to comfort him and help him recover. No, we didn't passionately cuddle or feed each other chocolate ice-cream, but instead I gave him my honest opinion about his results and how he wasn't working hard enough. I told him that he was going out too much, and that doing well in HL Math wasn't possible with minimal studying. Fast forward six months, and he came out with a solid 6 at the end of the IB Exams.

The beauty of having good friends is invaluable. They make you smile, laugh, and love. The quote that goes 'Friendship is like peeing on yourself: everyone can see it, but only you get the warm feeling that it brings!' (Robert Bloch) is so true. Don't seek quantity. One really good friend is better than three or four average ones. Spend time with people that you connect with, want to learn off, and genuinely enjoy conversing with. No, don't do it for the popularity aspect or seek people to validate your ego. You are better than that and you know it.

Your Squad

You will almost certainly develop a core group of friends within your IB classes. Try to be friends with students who have similar goals and aspirations as you, stay away from the trouble-makers and keep in mind that it's not 'cool' to be a total failing slacker. It's good to have a group with different genders, cultures, and nationalities. Being at an IB school means you are likely exposed to a myriad of cultures – make the most of this so you can enrich yourself with other perspectives.

With your closest group of IB friends, I suggest you guys keep a WhatsApp group or a Skype chat open together. Surprisingly, this makes it easier to motivate and help each other. There are no better comforting words to an IB student then 'I haven't started it either'. Studying with your close IB squad over digital mediums is also an invaluable practice if done correct.

Competition

The most important thing I can say about your in-class friendships is this: remember that the IB is not a competition amongst you. As in, marks are not standardized, certainly not in your classes. If you all deserve a grade 7, all of you will get a grade 7. Just because you get a very good mark on an assignment, does not mean that others cannot also get good marks. This means that there is a great incentive to help each other out and not withhold anything from each other.

I'm not saying copy and share your work; I am merely suggesting that you get the idea of 'competition amongst my peers' out of your head because there is no such thing. You should see your entire IB friend-group as one team, and you want everyone on that team to do well because you are not competing against each other.

So effectively that means you should study together. You should lend them your spare calculator if they forgot theirs. You should double-check the spelling and grammar in their IA if they ask you kindly. Within limits, you should have a very productive and co-operative friendship with your close IB friends.

Online Community

Undoubtedly, building strong IB friendships in your class will not be possible for everyone. Some of you may have fewer IB students at your school than there are fingers on your hands. Some of you may just find it hard making friends. Some of you may have some anxiety issues and would prefer to keep to yourself. This is where I am grateful that we live in the digital age and that there exist online communities to cater to anyone with an interest in anything.

Smartib App

As you probably know from the introduction of this book, smartib is a free iOS and Android app that I created over the last year and half. The app is essentially a social media app designed specifically for IB students, allowing candidates to create accounts and find other IB kids around the world. There is a well-organized forum where students can ask questions, but you can also 'follow' students with similar interests so you can see what they are up to.

At the time of publication, smartib is still undergoing huge updates including the ability to private inbox other students, and a huge live group-chat for IB kids. These are efforts to increase and better social communications between IB kids around the world. If you haven't already, I strongly recommend downloading the smartib app and checking it out right now.

Reddit IBO/ IBsurvival / Discord / Telegraph app

These are all alternative digital avenues for finding IB students around the world. The Reddit IBO subreddit is actually really helpful and insightful: (www.reddit.com/r/IBO).

Discord is the name of a chat program, and you can find the official IB channel via the Reddit page.

IBsurvival.com was once the only place to go and meet new IB students online. I used it quite a bit back in 2007 when it had less than a few thousand users. Recently it has undergone some less than ideal changes with regards to its moderators and changes to its files policy, but it is still worth checking out sometimes.

Take some time to do some research of your own into online IB communities. Hopefully, by the time you are reading this book, my smartib app will be the main IB online community and have most of IB kids already socializing and answering questions on it!

Whether online or in real-life, the friendship you develop during your IB years will be friendships you remember for a long time. There is a certain 'comradery' in knowing that you are all in this together, and the amount of support you get will be very comforting. It's kind of like you are all jumping into an abyss with friends from all around the world and you are all coming out together as a whole community. The IB and the exams will make you feel oddly closer to those already close to you. Don't take them for granted.

13. Time Management

(contributed article)

You probably have heard stories about how IB students have no life. I disagree; this is my life. Like many of you, I find myself juggling schoolwork, extra-curricular activities, friends, and unsatisfied parents. It came to a point when I just had to say "No" to certain activities that I absolutely love and "Yes" to the mountain of homework piling up on my desk, or in my MacBook, to be exact. So how do we determine when to say "Yes" and "No"?

Schoolwork is important, but so is the upcoming basketball game. Can you excel in both? Yes. But can you also fit in student council, Model United Nations (MUN), robotics, service projects, photography, chess, youth group, table tennis, and SAT classes? Probably not. The key word is to prioritize. Say "Yes" to activities that you are passionate about, challenge yourself to something new, and wholeheartedly to it. Say "No" to activities that are not meaningful to you, and do not blindly join boring activities just because your friends will be there. Although you may develop a new hobby once you join a club, if you know you will waste your whole afternoon in the martial arts club painfully wishing you were somewhere else, or will stay up until 2 am doing homework because you have three after school activities in a day, say no.

I kept my main activities every year throughout middle and high school: volleyball, basketball, student council, piano, and church. I also attended various other activities such as the school musicals, badminton, and service projects. Unfortunately, I had to sacrifice soccer, dance, and MUN. I still feel a hint of regret at not being able to do these things. I love group activities because I can meet other enthusiastic people and become more motivated to achieve certain goals. Sports games and other events brought excitement into my life, and gave me an overwhelming sense of accomplishment when they went well. As an emotional human being, I noticed that when I was in a good mood, I was more likely to be energetic and ready to tackle difficult assignments, especially those dreadful analytical essays.

How many activities should you join? Aim for at least three big projects, and participate in as many activities as possible when you still have the time and energy. Depending on your personality, you can lean towards group or individual activities, if you have a mix of both. Group activities are great for socializing while individual activities such as reading and playing the violin can be very refreshing. Fill out all your CAS (Creativity, Action, Service) forms and reflections as the activity is going on, because your life will be in chaos by senior year.

From endless lectures, you already know that time management is crucial and procrastination is deadly. It is especially evident as IB diploma students attempt to accomplish internal assessments, extended essays, language orals, Theory of Knowledge essays, exams, and the required CAS hours. What worked very well for me was to take a 15-minute snack break after I get home from after school activities, and then start on my homework right away. My concentration level would be very high and I could actually get a lot done before dinnertime. Once my brain switched to relaxation mode after dinner, it was much more difficult to focus again. Give it a try for a few days and see if it works for you. Instead of daydreaming on the bus, mentally list out your homework and the order you will do it in. This saves time and gives you a goal. All-nighters may work once in a while, but sleep deprivation will just lead to lower concentration levels and more all-nighters. Just remember, if you do not feel like doing work now, you will not feel like doing it later either.

The perfect balance between activities and IB varies among individuals, but there are a few universal tips. Remember, say

"Yes" to studying during study period, doing productive work instead of chatting to people on Facebook, and sleeping before midnight. Say "No" to messy desks, over-commitment, and any type of distraction that will cause procrastination. Life should never be extremely boring or painful. Just learn to say "Yes" and "No".

Parkinson's Law states that: "work expands so as to fill the time available for its completion"; this means that sometimes it is better to leave work for the last minute. My TOK presentation can serve as the perfect example. I was great at understanding TOK when we spoke about it in class, but when it came to creating the presentation I struggled. I worked on it for two months but most of the useful work was done the day before the exam in Luton airport, on napkins using my phone and airport internet. Now, how well did I perform? I got a 9/10 which allowed me to get a B in TOK and 3 bonus points. Don't get me wrong, most work left to the last minute won't get you a good grade and you should always try to get things done in advance, but it won't be possible with everything.

I had done research and asked for a lot of advice from my TOK teacher beforehand and each time I was told to re-plan and remake my Knowledge Issue. This allowed me to gain pertinent knowledge in my area of study and the way the TOK presentation works. This allowed me to finish my presentation in 4 hours once I had an approved Knowledge issue. Being good under pressure can help too, and you will be using that skill a lot in the IB, but you need to know when to use it and when to work in advance. The earlier you start working on something the better it will be. However, people and IB students have the tendency to go off topic and attempt to dazzle their examiners with bullshit (IB therefore I BS). Remember, as Parkinson stated, the more time you have the more work you will make for yourself. So be sure you know what you need to do (look at the grading scheme and ask your teachers) and only include what's necessary and occasionally a little extra.

78

Get this done fast, hand it in before it's due, get feedback and improve. This is the best way to maximise you time and improve your grade. The extended essay must simply be done. There's no time to think and ponder. Once you have finally chosen your subject and area of interest, put aside one week to develop your guiding question and create a plan. Review this with your mentor and improve on the structure during that week (this may include several meetings). Then put aside a second week (preferably during holidays) to work on the essay and its content. This should be an intensive week of data collection, processing and synthesising by the end of which your essay should be 70% done.

Starting from that week, meet weekly with your mentor and get through specific points in your essay. With about three hours of work a week on your essay and consistent modifications it should take you a month to finish your work. I was originally planning to write my essay on mathematics and computer algorithms, but at the end of the first year of IB I changed my subject and mentor, selecting computer sciences.

The problem was that I didn't take IB computer sciences. I started freaking out as I thought I was honestly screwed. I spent the summer holidays reading some books on computer sciences (the theory) and reviewed the course guides and grading schemes from the IB. Once back to school I met with my new supervisor and we quickly developed a question. I was later able to do most of the writing during October break and any changes after that were mainly re-edits. Despite starting late, I was able to still get an A in my Extended Essay.

This was possible because I had a strong plan and solid, well defined guiding question, a passion for my subject, and finally because I wrote the essay in a short well defined period of time and spent even more time improving it.

14. IB Efficiency and Self-Improvement

(contributed article)

The Pareto Principle, when applied to studying at school, states that roughly 80% of your results (achievements, good grades) come from 20% of your studying habits. This means that the biggest reasons behind you doing well on an exam or assignment will come from a limited time of studying. This is often an extremely difficult concept to grasp, because ever since you've entered high school your teachers and parents have told you to work long hours and slog it out.

The problem with this mentality is that you often end up spending 4-5 hours on topics that you already understand really well, and thus waste your time. Still, you go to bed that night thinking that since you spent 4 hours on something, you must have accomplished the task. This is simply not the case. The longer you work on a topic is not proportional to how well you know that topic. Instead, the smarter you work on studying a topic ensures your proficiency in it. What do I mean by smarter? I mean doing things like active studying, moving on when you're stuck, and talking closely with your teachers.

Here's a really good example of the Pareto Principle in action: to prepare for my SL Math Exams, I used to go through very long past papers, doing every single question and looking at the markschemes very closely. Now before the exams, this is something that you're going to have to do. It builds stamina, helps you understand the questions better, and builds comfort.

However, I had a problem with probability questions; I simply couldn't do them. After looking over my mock exams, my problem sets that my teacher had assigned, and my own workbook, I realized that there were a particular set of probability questions that I wasn't getting; those that had to do with expected value.

So, what did I do to get better? Well, I still continued doing full length past papers once a week to build stamina and get practice, but to really strengthen my weakness of probability, I firstly made custom problem sets for myself using the question bank filled with only probability questions. Then, I even narrowed those problem sets down to questions with only the topic of Expected Value. This allowed for smart, focused, weakness-based revision. I soon noticed an improvement in my results, and this was all down to working more efficiently and applying Pareto's Principle.

Don't Try to Do Everything at Once

I think that overexerting yourself is relevant to a lot of students because when you're surrounded by high-achieving individuals that are of the same age, you feel compelled to do stuff – and most of the time this is okay. You work hard, try new activities, and engage in healthy competition. But I feel as if it can be really harmful too.

Just yesterday, I heard some girl almost 'bragging' about how little sleep she got the other night. She was saying something like 'I had 5 hours of band practice, then I had to attend my MUN meeting, then I had a tutor for 2 hours, and then I had to do all my homework. Oh I slept at like 4am, I work soooo hard!!!'

I mean, don't get me wrong: doing stuff is good. But there's a limit, you know?

If we try to do everything, if we try to make everyone happy, and if we try to say yes to everything, we're missing out on some valuable time. We're missing out on time and energy that should be spent on ourselves.

How often do you spend time on self-reflection? How often do you analyze your strengths and weaknesses?

A common theme that I've noticed in so many successful people is the amount of time they spend taking care of themselves. This can be through meditation, running, reading, whatever; the point is that if you're not setting aside time to work on yourself, you're massively limiting your potential to grow.

In the IB, I think it's the same way. You must prioritize. You must find a way to maximize your output & productivity but at the same time you can't survive on four hours of sleep every night.

I know that when you're taking the IB this all sounds very abstract and meaningless, but please do take some time to self-reflect. In the long run, are you better off spending some time with your little sister who you're not going to see next year or should you attend a club meeting just so that you can put it on your CV.

99% of people will carry on their lives keeping themselves busy and doing meaningless activities. The 1% that succeed will be self-critical (and accountable), pursue activities that they are genuinely interested in, and aim to maximize happiness (and not wealth or status). You have the potential to do anything in this world, if and only if, you don't try to do everything.

That will surely lead to unhappiness and regret.

Self-Improvement

If you have plateaued at increasing your efficiency and feel like you are not improving, try going through this checklist quickly, which covers some of the aspects discussed in the previous chapters:

1. You Don't Want It Badly Enough

You say that you want to get better grades and that you're willing to sacrifice certain aspects of your life, but when it really starts to matter you don't walk the talk. This is the most common reason: people spend hours reading motivational articles and watching videos, but their inability to ever take action, or rather to only sustain action for the short-term, leads them to keep repeating the same mistakes.

How to fix this: Try to keep some system of accountability, by either telling someone that you're about to do something meaningful (and keeping them updated on your progress by sending them weekly emails), or another way would be to have a calendar filled with crosses when you achieve your goals for the day. This is surprisingly helpful, as you don't want to 'break' the crosses streak that is building up on your calendar.

2. You're Surrounded By Toxic People

They say that you are the average of the five people that you hangout the most with. Either way, if you're hanging around with slackers that keep claiming they 'have the potential' to do amazing but simply don't try, then you're doing it wrong. Or, maybe, that's the type of people you want to associate with. On the other hand, if you want to do well in school and are ambitious about your future, surround yourself with the right people. By this I don't necessarily mean the smartest; I mean people that bring positive energy to your life, people that help you out in times of need, and people that themselves are amazingly motivated to do great things with their education.

How to fix this: All up to you. Don't be afraid to completely disconnect with people that bring you down. Easier said than done.

3. You Are Being Stubborn

at throughout all of middle school, studying at the bus with your textbook open in one hand, a bag ...cetos lazily scrawled over your lap, and one Apple earphone plugged in might have gotten the job done, but it won't do for HL Math. You need to try new techniques that you may have previously totally dismissed. Take it from me: I was horrifically repulsed by the idea of meditating. I mean, what the hell is meditation? Now in college, I can't survive without it, and it's done wonders to my memory that has benefitted me enormously in my studies.

How to fix this: Venture out of your comfort zone, try new study techniques, and consult people that you look highly up-to and ask for their advice. If you don't try anything right now, you might regret it later.

4. You're Scared To Ask Questions

This is a really important one. People love to protect their big old ego; they're scared that if they ask a stupid question everyone will think they're not so smart or that they're inferior. It's all about status, after all, isn't it? Society has constantly drilled into us that our self-worth is based on how smart or good-looking we are relative to our peers. And it's all complete nonsense. People that actively seek out feedback, who ask questions because they genuinely want to better themselves and not for the sake of looking smart, do much better in the long run than their counterparts. Be vulnerable; don't be afraid to put your intelligence on the line. You're here to learn, and the best way to do that is to question absolutely everything.

How to fix this: I already addressed this above but something else that I'd recommend is to read the book 'Mindset' by Carol Dweck; it's an amazing read and it'll change the way you look at progress, especially in terms of your academic life.

5. You Are Too Comfortable

If you're really serious about improving yourself, whether that is academically or in any other aspect of your life, you should always strive to seek new uncomfortable situations. This is because when you're comfortable, you get stuck in a routine, that although may be getting you good grades and make you feel happy, is not ideal at all for bettering yourself. And trust me, there is no better feeling in the world than looking back and seeing how far you've come after genuinely having put yourself in new, vulnerable situations to learn something new.

How to fix this: Say yes to opportunities that are outside your comfort zone; aim to better yourself a little everyday by doing something that you're not used to at all.

6) You Need to Actively Change

This literally applies to anything you do in life. If you're not happy with the way things are going, find a solution. Don't just sit there and hope that things will get better. If you don't understand a term in your Physics class, and you're magically hoping that your teacher will omit it from that exam, you're screwed. Be active about learning; as I've mentioned above, ask questions, try something new, and don't be afraid to fail.

7) You're Not Taking Care of Yourself

You might be actively learning, trying out new things, pushing out of your comfort zone, asking tons of questions, but if you don't get enough sleep, keep yourself happy, exercise, and maintain your social wellbeing, nothing will get better. You only get one body: take care of it! If you're sleep deprived, nothing you learn will actually stick. This is especially true during exam season; it is absolutely vital that you keep yourself mentally refreshed! So many people just focus on studying 24/7, and that's just plain stupid. To do well academically, it is imperative that you keep yourself healthy.

How to fix this: exercise regularly, eat right, spend time with friends (before you start shouting at me that all of this can't be done- yes, it can, I did it myself) and make sure to remember that at the end of the day your mental health comes first.

15. Improving Memory

(contributed article)

Upon graduating from the IB, many current students at my previous school had countless requests for notes. This surprised me, truly it did. Why would someone ask for my notes, surely they would find them useless?

Think about it, what are notes? It's a summary of some text book, often riddled with spelling mistakes and abbreviations that make it almost impossible to read. So why would someone go through the trouble of deciphering my hand writing and reading bullet points of much better text books? I have always viewed notes as a retention tool, something that helps you remember things in the long run. But you don't remember better by reading over them, you remember by writing them. 80% (I may or may not be making that statistic up – hey, I am an IB student okay) of the benefits of creating notes comes from actually creating them: putting the pen to paper will help your retention of the information.

I know it's an unpopular opinion but I do suggest you create a large chunk of your notes by hand and not on a PC. Firstly you will be writing your exams on paper (unless you have the permission to use a word processor) hence you will be able to recall the information better during the exam. Secondly, it's much easier to draw diagrams and little graphics by hand than on a computer, and having graphs and pictures in your notes will help.

So why do notes help you remember better? It's a combination of different things. For example, if you were to read a text book, you might not be actively thinking about the information presented to you, but rather skimming over it and taking in the "words" rather than the concepts. If you are making notes, abbreviating into your own words, you are forced to process the information you are reading. This extra level of processing that happens in your brain creates more and stronger memories, ones that will last longer. Additionally, writing brings another dimension to learning. You are no longer simply thinking or reading, you are also creating and moving in the physical realm. The more senses you can associate with the learning process the easier it will be able to remember things.

Now in the future if you still have your notes, and you are reading over them you might notice that you remember things much faster then if you were to read the text book. This is because your mind has created a particular association with the notes you created, much like little "checkpoints" in your brain that are triggered causing old memories to come back.

Some of you might have been blessed with the best memory in the world: you learned something once and you will never forget it. Unfortunately most of us aren't so lucky. So if you are like me and consistently forget things, you should listen to this advice. I'll talk about a few techniques I've learned over the year on how to remember things better.

Don't simply read, actively read. That extra word "actively" makes the difference. Reading actively means that you are highlighting, writing into your book and really thinking about what you are reading. This last point might sound rather obvious; however trust me when I tell you it's far too easy to read but not actually take in the information. So be sure to stop every few paragraphs and reflect aloud on what you have read. Discuss with yourself the points you have gone over, even go online and do some further research on the subject.

The second point is to take notes, as mentioned in the previous chapter. I have gone over this before, however I want to emphasize it yet again: NOTES HELP. Make notes, even if you aren't going to read over them later. Having to process the information into your own words makes it more likely that you will remember said information. The combination of actually writing things down (do it by hand as your exams will be most likely hand written) and converting other people's words into your own helps with information retention.

Reviewing your material is yet another key way to improve your memory. When I talk about review, I don't simply mean doing a few hours of revision before the exams. Proper review entails that you take 15 min per subject every day to review your day's notes and class work. You should also put in addition to your homework, half an hour at the end of each week per subject to review the week's lessons.

This is the most interesting and exotic part of memory retention in my opinion. I have over time tested two techniques that have helped me with improving my memory; I don't know if this has been due to a placebo effect or that they actually helped, anyways here they come.

16. Writing IB Essays

You may think you know what an essay is. You may *think* you do.

IB essays test whether you can give a precise answer to a very precise question. IB essays also test whether you can use evidence and logic to support that precise answer. Keep that in your head because it seems simple, and is some ways it is, but it's too east to drift away from that concept. Your teachers will give you a method for writing essays. Almost any method can work – just hang onto the idea mentioned above: a precise answer to a precise question – with evidence and logic.

It can be very useful to think of the process backwards, to think about where you want to end up, and then how to get there. It's probably how you tackle the job of writing the essay. Therefore, this is something like what you do when told to write an essay:

Someone asks you a question – your overall answer is going to be the last paragraph or conclusion of the essay. You will have to support or prove that answer/conclusion, giving your evidence and your reasons – that will be the body of your essay, which leads up to that final paragraph. You'll have to start by discussing a few ideas and definitions to explain yourself – that will be the introduction which clears the way for the body of the essay.

So, the process should be: i) think of what your answer is to the question ii) think of the reasons/evidence/proof for that answer iii) plan the sequence of the ideas, check that they answer the question iv) write the essay.

In your school the teachers will hopefully teach you a method of writing essays. They will tell you it's the only or the best way to do it, and will demand you do it, and maybe even mark you down for not doing it their way. This is entirely reasonable, but only part of the truth. It's the International Baccalaureate – in other words, IBO needs to accept lots of different conventions and methods for doing work in many different countries. If there is a single correct method for doing anything, then the IBO must explicitly say that – in the case of essays, they don't.

The Introduction

This is really important – in fact this is probably the most important aspect of the essay. Examiners will tell you that they basically have a very good idea what your final mark will be after they have just read the first paragraph. For example, in Language A, if somebody asks, 'Do you think love is an important theme in the texts you have studied', you're going to say which kinds of love you're going to focus on – love of country, parents, animals, sports, etc. You will want to define what you mean by 'important'.

Always re-check your first paragraph. You should absolutely never misspell the name of an important text/person/character/country – the examiner will have a hard time believing that you are not an idiot. Under no circumstance do you want to give them that benefit of the doubt because that will then be on their mind the rest of the time.

So, in the introduction, be sure to define any central key terms you will be using throughout your essay. Mention what texts/areas/periods/ you will be focusing on. Outline and signal the points you will be discussing. It really is that simple.

The Body

The body of the essay is where you discuss the points you are trying to prove, which lead to an answer to the question. In general, in literature and social sciences, there are usually no 'right answers' that the examiner will be waiting for you to produce – although there are certainly 'wrong answers'. The examiner probably doesn't care much for your opinion's – they are only concerned with the criteria that has been given to them.

As long as you are good at arguing your point across, it does not really matter which side of the argument you choose. What matters is whether you can explain your ideas, and whether you can find evidence to support them. Three good points is usually a good amount – for an essay or a presentation or commentary. Two points may look like you don't have enough ideas, and four solid points may mean you don't have enough time to go into enough detail.

Thus, the body needs to i) say what the point is ii) explain it iii) give support and evidence and iv) show how it helps answer the actual question.

Conclusion

If you have done the previous work right, then this becomes very simple – it's just your overall answer to the question in the final paragraph. It's where you essentially say 'having looked at these three points, it becomes evident that the answer to the question is…' So you end up with a complex answer, but the examiner understands how you got there, and they see your reasons. They also understand you have chosen what to say out of many possibilities you were aware of.

So, in the conclusion: i) make sure you've got an explicit answer to the question ii) explain/show how that answer is supported by the three points you discussed and iii) check for mistakes – you don't want to leave a bad impression with carelessness.

17. Mastering the IB Presentation

There will be plenty of times when you will be required to do an IB presentation – in Language A, Language B, TOK, Group 4 projects etc. Presenting is a set of skills that you must learn – organising ideas, and finding vivid ways to show them. In this section, we will try to go over some preliminary bits of advice that should help you maximize your marks on general IB presentations.

First, find a topic that actually interests you – this way you are more likely to do better research and you will be more lively talking about it. Obviously there will be limits to this depending on what subject you are presenting for, but most of the time you will have some degree of flexibility on what you wish to talk about.

Just as with the perfect IB essay, the perfect IB presentation also has a beginning, middle and an end. The beginning should have some kind of captivating hook to get the audience engaged: like a puzzle. You should also make an effort to inform your audience *exactly* what you are going to talk about. So, you should say, 'I'm going to argue x, y, z…'. If your audience knows what you are going to focus on, they will follow much better. Also, if possible, try to make the presentation relevant to your audience from the start – give them a reason as to why they should listen.

The middle of the presentation will be the points which are the heart of what you're about and what you want your audience to think about. When you're preparing, try to put each point in a very clear single sentence. Look at your ideas from different points of view. What are the problems with or arguments against what you are saying? Make sure to show the transition between each point. If using multiple speakers, this might be a good point to choose a different speaker to address that point. Make sure to vary your method of presenting for each point as students tend to drift off after 2-3 minutes.

The end of your presentation is arguably the most important part. It's what is in the teacher's mind when they give you the mark. You need to make sure to wrap it all up. Ensure that the audience got the points you were making and give them a conclusion – so they see what the purpose of the presentation was and why it mattered. You should also open up your presentation to your audience and if allowed, give them a chance to express their opinion or arguments. At the very end, you will need to give them the answer to whatever the hook of the presentation topic was.

How to Present

It's important to think of the presentation as not just talking. It needs to really engage the audience. Think of it as a series of images, pictures, diagrams, maps, film clips and interactive materials. What you and your group might do is talk about them, comment, and then explain connections and implications. Using visuals also stops the audience looking at you – which makes it more interesting for them (no offence) and less panic-inducing for you.

Use the Criteria

This is probably the most important take-away from this chapter on IB presentations. For the love of god, please consult the grading criteria upon which you will be assessed for that specific presentation. Remember, the criteria is all that any examiner has, including your teacher. Even if you have an 'excellent' presentation (in the sense that it was exciting and interesting and everyone enjoyed it), you could still score poorly if you didn't tick the boxes on the assessment criteria. I see this happen time and time again with students.

For example, if the TOK criteria says 'identify a knowledge question relevant to a real life scenario' then you better damn well do those two things to get the full 5 marks. You need to i) identify explicitly a 'knowledge question' and ii) explicitly identify a real life scenario. Failure to do either will prevent you from getting top marks.

You have specific assessment criteria for TOK, Language A, Language B, Group 4 and so on. They are not the same, and in fact the differences are very important. Get your hands on the relevant criteria and turn them into a bullet point list or checklist. You may even want to hand in a copy of this to your teacher so they can see that you know what you had to do.

18. IB Exam Revision [Part 1]

Preparing for the final exams can be a daunting task. Once the examination timetable is published your first exam date will remain cemented in your mind. Although there are hundreds of ways to revise for the examinations, many are largely ineffective and far too time consuming. In this chapter I will give you some general guidelines for how to best revise for your final exams.

Time Management

Having me preach to you about the importance of time management is perhaps hypocrisy at its best. For me it was not until I got into university that I really started to understand how effective time management can be. If you are one of the few who has mastered the skill at an early age then consider yourself lucky. This is an invaluable ability that you will use regularly throughout your life.

One of the great rewards of undertaking the IB challenge is that you will have the opportunity to learn amazing time-management skills. The key to good time management is not just writing up a good schedule, but also imposing consequences when you fail to adhere to that schedule. For example if you promised to revise biology for 45 minutes a day every weekday and then you only manage to do 15 minutes on one of days, you must make sure you catch up on the remaining half an hour the day after.

When Do I Start?

I had a teacher who once told the class (with 4 months remaining until final exams), "I hope your revision is going well... and if there are still some of you that haven't started revising, well you are already behind." Hearing those words I got uncomfortably nervous and stressed. Not only had I not begun revising, I didn't even know where to start. Several weeks passed as I procrastinated even more and eventually "mock exams" came around. I didn't study much, except for glancing over a few past papers from the previous year. Luckily, it turned out that some of the "mock exams" were in fact last year's actual examinations. Nonetheless, I didn't have a good feeling about the whole thing and my grades reflected this – got a 36 overall with a 4 in HL Mathematics. This was a real wake up call as my university offer was given on the condition that I get a minimum of 40 points overall and a 7 in HL Mathematics and Economics. I feared the worst.

With less than a month to revise and no quick solution in sight, I was probably justified in my distress. Some of my friends had been "revising" since the beginning of winter break. I was too busy partying and procrastinating. With less than a month to go until exams I knew that this month would make or break me. I quickly made a demanding exam schedule and started it the following day. For a whole month I practically lived in a cave, having deactivated Facebook and deleted Skype. I read, breathed and lived revision. The only thing that kept me going was a voice in the back of my head telling me "you did nothing for two years, the least you can do is work mercilessly for one month, and then it will be all over."

The whole point of that little story is not to suggest that you should only leave a month for revision. It was simply to demonstrate to you what you will have to go through if you do leave revision so late. I was never one to miss a party – there was no way I could give up weekends, and sports, and all my hobbies just so that I could start revision many months in advance. I left revision too late, but, I paid the price. Whatever choice you make, you need to realise that you will have to bear the consequences when your actual exam preparation comes around.

There is no ideal time to start revising. That being said, you should never leave less than a month, and you would probably be wasting your time starting revision any sooner than 3 months before exams. Some of you may seem confused as to why I am suggesting that you don't study too much, but that's not what I am saying. There have been studies done that show how students can reach the "peak" of their revision too early, and have a "meltdown" before actual exams. This usually happens to students that start revising nearly a year in advance. By revising too much in advance you may run the risk of failing to recall the earliest information and start to panic.

Perhaps the golden rule to IB exam revision can be worked out logically. If you still have assignments to finish that will be graded by the IB, it's probably safe to say that you should not even think about starting revising. Your Internal Assessment is far more important than early revision so make sure you get that out the way first. Once all your work has been sent off you can drop everything else and just focus on revising for your exams. Always remember your priorities: first get all the IA out of the way, and then you can centre all your attention on revision.

The IB is too demanding for you to be starting revision early. With all the tests, assignments, sports meetings, CAS reports and homework that you will have on your hands, you will not be able to begin preparing too much in advance. Don't forget however that all the tests and coursework that you are doing is a form of revision. It's not the best, but at least you are doing something to reinforce your knowledge of the subject. So don't think you are doomed if you haven't been revising out of a textbook with a month to go before exams. You have been revising "indirectly". At least that's what I told myself to be able to sleep at night.

Mock Examinations

Most schools will administer "mock" examinations several weeks or months prior to the actual exams. This is not really a test of your knowledge and how well you will perform on the actual exam. It's more to get you familiar with examination conduct and protocol. You will need to get used to arriving punctually, having the right materials, and following exam rules and regulations.

Nonetheless, I suggest you make full use of your mock exams and treat them almost as if they were the real deal. You will be able to see what you would achieve if you had sat the real exam and not done any revision. Thus, it is kind of a test of how focused you were in class throughout the year. For most of you this experience will be a wake-up call.

Once your mock exam results come out don't just glance at the grade and move forward. Find out where you went wrong and where you could have done better. Although these exams are graded by your teachers, it doesn't mean the marking will be much different when done by examiners elsewhere. Look for places where you lost marks due to silly mistakes and try to work on these mistakes before your real examination.

One final note on mock examinations. It is no hidden secret that most schools use last year's real paper as the current year's mock paper. Don't think that you are a genius for figuring this out. This has been a tradition in most schools, however some now started to come up with new material. Nonetheless, if your mock exam paper happens to be a past paper that you have already worked on yourself then don't feel guilty or feel like you didn't deserve the grade you got. If you did well that just shows that your work with past papers has been worthwhile. You were able to apply the material again, meaning you probably learnt something along the way. If you still did poorly despite having seen the paper and the markscheme beforehand then you have reason to worry.

19. IB Exam Revision [Part 2]

What do I revise?

You should by now realise that you will not be devoting an equal share of revision time to each subject. Some subjects you may not even bother with until perhaps a few weeks before the final exam. Other subjects you may like to start revising several months in advance. This will all depend on what your strengths are, as well as what your aims are.

For example; my IB results needed to coincide with my university offer from Oxford – I didn't really care about much else. This meant that I needed a 40 overall, 7's in HL Mathematics and HL Economics, as well as 6's in all of my remaining subjects. As soon as I learnt of this offer, I immediately outlined my problem areas. I knew that getting a 7 in HL Mathematics was by far my greatest weakness. I had never gotten a 7 in any test, and was probably averaging out a 5 overall. I felt uncomfortable with a large portion of the material. I also knew that getting a minimum of 6 in HL Geography and SL English should not be too big of a problem. I felt very comfortable with the Geography material, and my IA for English seemed good enough. Having gone over all of this in my head, I began to formulate how I will go about revising. I ended up spending more than 50% of my revision on Mathematics (doing a past paper almost every other night), then 30% on Economics (because I couldn't take any risks as I had to get a 7) and the rest of time I divided equally amongst the remaining subjects.

This may come as a shock to a lot of you. How can one spend more than half of their revision time on just one subject? Instinctively, you would want to divide your time equally amongst the six subjects giving you an equal chance of doing well in all of them. This is not the correct way to think. You need to identify your weaknesses and base your revision around this. If you are borderline failing Chemistry and sailing through Business Management, then focus all your attention on getting through the Chemistry material. You may not enjoy it as much as BM but it's by far more important to you and your overall grade.

Figure out what your problem areas are by looking at your predicted grades and talking to your teachers to check where you stand in terms of their predictions. More importantly, you should know by now what your aims and objectives are. Do you need a minimum of a 6 in this subject for university or university credits? Do you need a 7 in this in order to fulfil the requirements? Once you work out what you are aiming for then make sure to focus your energy on this specifically. If you don't have any set aims and you are just trying to get the greatest points total then your task may be slightly easier. Find out your where your Achilles heel lies and focus on this and this alone.

How Do I Revise?

Although there are a multitude of methods to revise for the actual exams, you need to be careful and avoid doing redundant tasks. Out of all the possible methods that are out there, I highly recommend you try to focus your revision around past papers. For a full detailed explanation of this method please refer to the specified chapter on Past Papers.

I know that this method may not work for everyone. Perhaps you made great notes throughout the year or you enjoy learning from the syllabus and the textbook. Nonetheless, more often than not the most successful IB candidates will tell you that they revised primarily with the help of past papers and markschemes.

If you still insist on studying from textbooks and notes, I recommend you cover some basic study tips. For example, some subjects such as biology may require more 'visual learner' skills – using your eyes and memory to recall the information. I know some students get very creative with this process and create highly effective 'mind maps' and 'word association' memory tools. I guess the theme here is sticking to the revision method that you know works for you the best. If you don't think you have one, I highly suggest you get cracking on past papers.

No matter what method you choose, I highly recommend that your revision remains active. By this I mean you are constantly writing, making notes, and writing again. Although lying in the grass with a book to cover your face from the sun sounds like a good plan, you are wasting your time. Sit at a desk, grab some plain white paper, and make good use of your pen and pencil. You are twice as likely to remember what you are revising if you are constantly writing and not just reading.

Some of you may find that study groups work well for particular subjects. I myself found it extremely useful to work together on a maths paper with another person, or to discuss economics material in a group. Choose your groups wisely though. Avoid students who are far more advanced than you and avoid friends that seem like they attend revision sessions more for the social aspect rather than actual studying. The point is that if you find revising or working through past papers with a group of equally motivated peers useful then by all means proceed with that.

You will probably have a good week or two of no school before your examinations begin so make full use of that period. Make sure each day is productive and that you set yourself mental tasks to complete every day. Don't be alarmed but you should probably be aiming to get at least 7 hours of pure revision done every day that week. This isn't really asking that much given that you probably haven't been doing much revision all year.

Don't panic if you come across something during your revision that you have never seen before. Chances are it probably isn't in the syllabus anymore or maybe you just missed it out in class. Ask your friends or your teacher for advice. You shouldn't spend hours and hours stuck on one section or problem – remember this should be revision and not first-time learning.

Another common mistake made during the revision period is setting yourself goals that are simply beyond your reach. No one expects you to revise for twelve hours a day straight, sleep for eight and leave four hours for washing/pooping /eating. It shouldn't have to come to that. You should be studying hard but also leaving a little time to relax and recover. Remember that there is a huge amount of resources available for you to aid in your revision.

20.IB Exam Revision [Part 3]

Cramming: The Night Before

No words of advice or comfort can really help ease your pre-exam stress and make you relax the night before your first examination. You will remember that date for a long time. For most of you, this is probably the first official externally graded examination that you take (unless you've done GCSEs or SATs). This can be a scary notion but you just need to realise that in a matter of a few weeks all of this will be over and you will embark on the longest holiday of your teenage life.

Now, what should you be doing the night before an exam? Well, as a golden rule, you should restrict your revising only on material for which you will be examined the following day. This means if you have a math exam tomorrow, you should be doing just math today – not biology which you have in a weeks' time or something like that. You need to keep the subject fresh and familiar in your mind – focus all your energy on it the night before and hopefully you will wake up with most of it still in your head.

Now, what about cramming? There is a heated debate as to whether cramming even works. Some say that having late night cram sessions is not only ineffective, but that it can put you in unnecessary stress and increase your chances of "going blank" the following day. Others will tell you that cramming is the best form of revision, and everything you stuff into your brain the night before just spills on your exam paper the next morning. Then there are also those who will tell you that cramming works – but you should not do it because you are not learning long-term, you are merely memorizing stuff in the short-term which you will probably forget in a weeks' time. Those people are missing the point.

From a personal viewpoint, cramming the night before an IB examination was helpful, but only to a certain extent (and only for certain subjects). For example, I found that cramming popular mathematic proofs was extremely helpful, however cramming an English novel was not. Use your common sense a little when it comes to cramming. More importantly, don't overdo it. Your sleep and nutrition can play a large role in your examinations, so make sure you are getting a minimum of six hours of sleep most of the days. Exceptions can be made when you have an exam the following day, and then after that you have a day or two break from exams for recovery – in that scenario I have seen some students even pull off near all-nighters.

Disappointment: The Morning After

However well your exam went, you are more than likely to come out feeling rather disappointed. This is natural. If you come out of the exam room very cheery and happy that usually means that either you have been very lucky and really aced it, or you really messed up a question or two because you misunderstood what was being asked. Either way, the most important thing to remember after every examination is to move on. Don't hang around outside the exam halls asking all your friends what they answered or what they thought of a certain question. The exam is over. Whatever you say or do after is not going to change what you wrote on that paper or the outcome of the exam. You need to revise for your other papers.

This is one of the biggest mistakes I see students make when it comes to revision. Instead of studying for the next paper, they waste time talking to their friends and trying to figure out how they got this or that answer, or what they wrote about in their essay. You are likely to get even more disappointed and discouraged if you waste time asking your friends what they wrote down only to find out that your answer was totally different. After you have just sat an examination, just go home as fast as you can and focus on the next one.

Moreover, if you have finished the last paper for a certain subject, then make sure you get that subject totally out of your head. Clear all the notes and papers for that subject out of the way and pretend that you don't even know what it is. Instead of doing six subjects, you are now only doing five. It is of vital importance that you make the transition from one subject to the next as smooth as you can as the exam schedules can be very hectic.

Method of Elimination: A Technique

One factor that separates the more successful exam candidates from the others is that the they have picked up certain examination techniques along the way. One of these is a revision technique by which you use a process of elimination to make an educated guess as to what might show up on the next paper. Let me give you an example: when I sat my HL Economics exam, Paper 1 had a big question on monopolies, but neither Paper 1 nor 2 had anything on negative externalities. I made an educated guess that there would be a big question on negative externalities on the Paper 3, with little emphasis on monopolies. This was indeed the case that year.

You can do this for almost any paper. Each subject has its key syllabus areas on which students should be examined. This is perhaps more true for Group 3, 4 and 5 subjects than the others. You can use the process of elimination to make a clever guess as to what could potentially show up on the next paper having already sat the first one. Discuss this with your friends as they probably have a similar inkling. This technique, combined with cramming, can practically make you an overnight expert on an area with which you were previously not that comfortable.

Last Minute Revision

You need to make full use of the last few moments before you enter the examination room. Find a nice quiet place to quickly run through key points and get any last minute cramming done. Avoid large groups of people as you will probably not be able to concentrate that well. You should probably even revise in the car/bus ride to the examination place. Just don't waste any valuable time that you have on useless distractions.

21. The Power of Past Papers

I'm sorry to disappoint you but if you have come here looking for free past papers and markschemes you are out of luck. At the same time, I wish to congratulate you because that kind of "I-need-past-papers" mentality is exactly what you need. If you have flipped through to this chapter in hopes of finding out where to get past papers and how to use them, then you can pat yourself on the back because you are now one step closer to getting 7's in your subjects.

If you have been reading this guide carefully then you should know just how much I have stressed the importance of past papers. Let me put it to you this way. If Internal Assessment takes around 25% of final IB grade, then your experience and practice with past papers could determine around half of what your final IB grade will be. The remaining 25% is down to a mixture of determination, natural academic ability and luck. Past papers are everything when it comes to acing your examinations.

Once again, to truly understand the power of past papers, we need to think logically. The syllabuses for most subjects have been written many years ago. The IB examinations are written to test your knowledge and grasp of the syllabus material. Thus there is only so much that they can possibly ask. If you look through past papers over and over again you are bound to see major similarities. Once again, the degree of similarity will vary across subjects, but nonetheless it is a fair generalisation. Think of it this way: there is a set amount of information you need to learn and the IBO wants to test your knowledge with respect to this information. Every year they will ask questions to test this knowledge. Surely there are only so many different ways they can test you. Eventually they start to run out of original questions.

Luckily for you, this has already happened. Look at the grade above you; they arguably were worse off. Similarly, the grade below you is better off. Why? Because yet another year of modern IB examinations has gone by. That means another set of past paper questions and markschemes has been made available. Consider yourself lucky that you have so much access to past papers and markschemes because ten years ago this was certainly not the case.

At the top major UK universities (including Oxford and Cambridge) you will find it impossible to get your hands on any markschemes. Past examinations are usually available (and even that can be a hassle), but markschemes are non-existent. The reasoning for this is quite simple to understand. The universities don't want students to simply digest the markschemes without learning the material properly. It levels out the playing field and makes the competition for top marks fiercer. Luckily for you the IB does not have this policy. Past papers and markschemes are recommended by the IBO and made available − albeit at a monetary cost.

Where do I get them?

The simple answer to this is anywhere you can. If you are amongst the lucky few then it can be the case that your school has an abundance of money and resources and will readily supply you with past papers and markschemes because they know how valuable they are. On the other hand, you may be at a school that lacks the financial muscle to buy these for students and is honest enough to not photocopy any. Nonetheless the first place you need to go to is your school. Your teachers, the library, your IB coordinator − basically anyone that might be able to help you. At some schools, students have access to nearly all available past examinations however the teachers may restrict what they give out because they may use them as future mock examinations. Even if the papers are covered in cobwebs and in a dusty old closet, make sure to get them out and look for more.

If that route fails, your next best option would probably be to go to the one place that has the answers to almost everything; the Internet. Be aware that there are several problems with this approach. First of all the IB strictly forbids any independent persons to host past papers and markschemes on the Internet and they regularly hunt down and threaten anyone who doesn't follow these rules. If you are lucky enough to find a website that does host past papers then it's unlikely to be there in a few weeks' time.

The last option you have is the most hassle-free: buying past papers and markschemes directly from the IBO website. Now don't get me wrong. I am against spending any more money on what is already a very expensive program. Nor do I understand why the IB would charge students more for additional "information."

What I strongly recommend you do is round up ten or so classmates that are interested in getting past papers and markschemes for a particular subject. If you each chip in, then together you can buy a copy from the official IBO past paper provider (the Follett IB store). Once you have all the papers you need you can share the papers between each other because they will be made available in a downloadable pdf format. Additionally, once you're done with your exams you can sell the papers off to the grade below.

All in all, you should never be spending more money on past papers then you would on a textbook – and past papers are technically far more valuable than any textbook (in my honest opinion). You need to get your hands on these papers, one way or another.

How many?

Although I usually urge you do more past papers in rough rather than one or two thoroughly, this approach also has its limitations. A good general approximate that I recommend is doing at least five years worth of examinations (both May and November papers). This adds up to ten separate examinations – which is a considerable amount of practice. Of course this will vary from subject to subject. For example for Group 1 topics, there is very little point in looking at more than 3 years worth of exams whereas for HL Mathematics you wouldn't do yourself any harm working through ten years of examinations if you really want that 7. A good rule to follow is to make sure you do enough past papers so that you start seeing repeat questions. Only then will you become comfortable and familiar with what the questions ask you to do.

Avoid going too far back into the database if you know there has been a serious change in syllabus/exam structure. For example, the HL Economics Paper 1 exam used to be multiple choice questions a decade ago. There is little point in looking at too many of those multiple-choice papers because you no longer have to sit such a paper. That being said, just because there has been a slight change in method of examination doesn't mean you should ignore the papers totally.

There are few feelings worse than having just sat an exam where one of the questions was incredibly similar to a past paper that you decided not to do. I highly doubt you can feel overly confident going into an examination if you haven't taken your chance to do all the past papers you could get your hands on (or at least glance over them properly). Make sure you don't have this regret – do enough past papers.

Past Papers vs. Markschemes

Some of you may be asking what's more important, the past paper or the markscheme? They are both of equal importance and you can't really have one without the other. There is no point in running through paper after paper if you have no way to check if your answers are even remotely correct. Similarly, you cannot just flick through random answers in the markschemes if you have no idea what the question was asking (unless, that is, the markscheme has the questions included).

Ultimately, you need have both the past paper and the markscheme for every examination that you are interested in. You will undoubtedly spend more time with the markscheme than you will with the past paper because you will want to see exactly what examiners are looking for. Nonetheless, get the past papers as well in case you want to do a practice examination or want to get a "feel" for the structure of the exam.

How do I "do" the past paper?

Contrary to what your teachers may have told you, it is not a crime to have the markscheme with you whilst you are answering questions from a past paper (sometimes!). This is one of the best forms of revision and is a method that is severely underused by students.

Ideally, you would want to complete each paper properly in the time set and only then get out the markscheme to see what mistakes you made. But we don't live in an ideal world. You don't have the time to sit 3-hour mock examinations for tens of papers in 6 different subjects and then go through each one with the markscheme. Your revision doesn't even really start until all the assessment is sent off so you will at best have a month or two of pure revision.

So what's the best thing to do once you have obtained the papers and the markschemes? Well, it will largely depend on you and what works for you individually. Personally, I found that for subjects such as Economics and Geography, I needed the markscheme near me as I was answering the questions from the past papers. I would have a scrap piece of paper next to me as well, glance at the question, jot down a rough answer, and then check with the markscheme what I missed out.

For Mathematics and Physics however, I found that by looking at the answers before I fully finished the question I was cheating myself. As a result I usually kept the markscheme away until I was totally stumped or found some sort of answer. The key thing to keep in mind is that you need to be constantly writing. Don't fool yourself into thinking you can go and lie down on your couch, past paper in one hand, markscheme in the other. Your revision needs to be active.

From my experience, I found that writing bullet-point scrap answers for past paper questions helped me learn the material much more than simply pondering over the answer and glancing at the markscheme. Remember what you are ultimately aiming for: to understand the material and be able to answer the question to the examiner's expectations. Your work with past papers and markschemes should make you feel more confident. If you pick up a past paper and are in total fear of what they ask, then clearly you are not yet prepared.

Don't underestimate the power of this technique. Markschemes are everything when it comes to scoring 7's in your subjects. Not only do they provide model answers but there is also a clear breakdown for the examiners for when to award marks. You have at your disposal everything that makes for a perfect examination. The closer you get to this perfection, the closer you will get to that grade 7. You will learn what it takes to make your paper worthy of a high mark. Learn to speak the examiner's lingo. Look for key words and phrases, memorize certain model definitions, and learn to give them what they are looking for.

By the time I was midway through my exams I had past papers and markschemes all over the place along with the model answers I wrote myself. The coffee table, the bedroom, the bathroom, the kitchen – everything and everywhere was covered with past papers. When you surround yourself with this information, you are less likely to forget it. By constantly consulting the past papers and markschemes you ensure that you will not be surprised by anything that could come up in the real examination.

SL/HL

Some of you may wonder whether there is any sense in going through past papers at a level which you do not necessarily do. This is at times fine if you are a Higher Level student looking to get a greater grasp of the questions and the syllabus, but I would not recommend that you go through Higher Level papers if you are a Standard Level student. You will not be "challenging yourself". You will probably just get confused and frightened because you won't be able to answer most of the questions. For example, I avoided looking at HL Physics papers because I found the SL ones challenging and adequate enough. That being said, I got too familiar with most of the HL Geography papers available so I started to go over a few SL papers (which was ok because the gap between SL and HL was not that great). Use your common sense and don't waste your time doing papers that are of no use to you.

IB Past Papers Petition

Granting students access to the past papers has been a mission of mine for the past decade. So much so that I started a petition that asks the IBO to release all the materials for all students. I believe this is the only fair thing to do and I explain why in this change.org petition, which I have linked here:

www.change.org/p/international-baccclaureate-organization-make-past-papers-and-markschemes-freely-available-smartib

You can also find it by searching chang.org for the 'IB past papers petition'. Please if you could read the petition and sign it, it would be one step closer to getting all future students access to these essential materials.

The point of this chapter was to make you appreciate the potential that past papers and markschemes offer. The most successful IB candidates nowadays heavily rely on past examination questions simply because it is an unbeatable strategy. Your teachers will probably disagree that learning from past papers and markschemes is a more effective study technique than learning from textbooks/notes but they have not done the exams themselves. Trust me on this one. Unless you have done absolutely as many past papers as you possibly can you will not be ready to sit the examinations and get that grade 7. I cannot stress this enough but I trust you have enough good judgement to see the logic behind this.

22.Examination Technique [Part I]

Although you should keep in mind that you need specific revision techniques for each individual subject, there remains much to be said about examination technique in general. Your success in the exams will not only rely on how well prepared you are in terms of the material, but also how well you perform under pressure. To deal with this you will need to master a few exam techniques. Most of them are simple, but nonetheless are often forgotten or severely underestimated.

Time Management

You need to be able to allocate your time proportionally across the entire duration of the exam. This includes taking off a few minutes from the beginning for reading and the end for proofreading. Whatever time you devote to actual writing and working out should be spaced out across the whole exam. Luckily, the IB have made your task even simpler as they now indicate how many points each question and sub-question is worth. For most papers this is the same year in year out however pay close attention to this as it will decide how many minutes you will need to spend on the question. If it takes you less time to answer than you had anticipated, then move on to next question as you may need that extra time.

You absolutely must, and under no exceptions, finish your exam from beginning to end. If you have not answered all the questions that were required of you then you can consider your grade 7 a missed opportunity. Once the examiner sees that you have left questions at the end blank, this immediately sends out a signal that you have mismanaged your time. This mistake is made every year by countless bright students and the only reason for it is poor organization and time use – something that is not expected from the best candidates.

There is absolutely no reason why you should not have enough time to finish the exam. I hear this excuse all the time but the truth is you did have enough time, you just didn't use it wisely. It's one thing to leave a question blank because you just had no idea how to answer it – which is something I also highly discourage. But it's a totally different matter if you didn't answer the last few questions because you messed up your timing.

Command Terms

These 'command terms' are specific words and phrases that the IB like to use in their exam questions. The IB examiners are not just trying to grade you on your knowledge of the subject, but they want to test your ability to answer the question that they have set out for you.

This is not something that is unique to the IB examinations. At university, and also in some job applications, you will be tested on your ability to really understand what is being asked. There is no point in answering how something happened if the question asked why did it happen. Get used to reading questions carefully and answering accordingly because this is a skill that you will reuse often.

Again, your success at identifying and answering these command terms will largely depend on your practice with past papers. That being said, no amount of preparation can spare you from being careless. For this reason make sure to double-check what is being asked. If time is available then I even recommend you highlight or underline the command term so that you don't forget what it is you need to answer. There's nothing worse than writing an answer explaining something when you were simply asked to define it.

A full list and explanation of command terms can be found in the syllabus/subject guide for the subject in question. These can be found online, or by asking your teacher. The terms differ from subject to subject. Please make sure you understand the command terms well before you go into the exams.

Extra Materials

Along with your lucky charms and favourite pen I strongly advise that you bring in a well-functioning clock in order to be able to manage your time properly. This varies amongst personal taste but I know that some like to have wrist watches, while some bring digital clocks, and I have even seen some bring countdown timers that were preset to countdown the exam duration. You need to keep in mind that although there may be already clock in the exam room you could be assigned a seat all the way in the back. Perhaps your eyesight isn't as great as you thought it was and as a result you struggle to see the time. Don't take any of these chances. Bring some sort of time device with you.

I always have a little bit of paranoia when it comes to calculators malfunctioning in exams so I strongly recommend that you bring a spare calculator (not necessarily the graphing one) or at least a spare set of batteries for the calculator-based exams. It goes without saying that you need a spare pen or two just in case the one you have runs out. Also, try to bring a set of highlighters because you can use these to remind yourself of the key terms in a question as discussed before in this chapter.

Answer the Whole Question and Nothing but the Question

This is self-explanatory. When answering any question on the IB exams you must make sure you address the exact phrasing in the question and give the examiner exactly what he/she is looking for. For all my examinations, I brought along a highlighter or two so that I could highlight key words in the question sentence. For example, if a math question stated "give the answer in cm^3" I would highlight the cm^3 part. I know that this might sounds a little pointless and a waste of time but you would be surprised to see how many candidates "forget" certain parts of the question. One common example is when a question asks you to "explain why" and you write an excellent essay on "how". By highlighting the "explain why" part you will significantly reduce the chances of this kind of slip up.

There is usually absolutely no reason to write more than what is required. If the question is worth two marks this means the examiner is probably looking for two key points – no more, no less. You don't have time to be writing everything you know. You need to pick the most valuable bits of information and keep to your own time limit. There are no "bonus" points and you will not get extra credit for writing what is not required. Remember, the key is to write efficiently and aim for maximum marks with minimum nonsense.

Less is More – Usually

There are a few exceptions to the above paragraphs. If, in the unlikely scenario that you stumble upon a question you don't how to fully answer, then sometimes (very rarely!) writing something that you do know on the topic might give you a few marks. This technique is very beneficial if used wisely, but it can also be very risky and damaging to your time if you abuse it. I can give you a good example. Suppose you get a "define" question worth two marks. This usually means you need to give two concrete points in order to get full marks. Let's suppose that you could only remember one. Whereas normally I would suggest that you not waste your time and just move on the next question, there will be times when a little bit more 'filler' might get you that other mark. Either expand on your first point or throw in some other information that could, maybe, give you the remaining mark (like adding an example).

Remember that directly you will not get marked down for writing more. Indirectly, you always run the risk of losing valuable time. There is a general belief that examiners will only read the first few points you make and ignore the rest if you haven't hit the nail on the head yet. Personally, I find that this notion is too general to apply to every examiner in every subject. Your best bet is to keep writing "educated guesses" until you think you have good odds at getting most of the marks. You won't lose marks, but you might not gain any either. Remember that you are facing a balancing act – writing more BS versus having more time to answer later questions.

23.Examination Technique [Part II]

Give Yourself Space

One of the first things you should do when you sit at your desk is carefully lay out all your materials. You don't want to be doing a three-hour examination curled up uncomfortably on a tiny working space. Place the examination paper on one side and the fill-in answer booklet next to it. Arrange your pencil case and all of your materials somewhere neatly in the corner. Make sure that your workspace is not one giant mess or else this could reflect negatively on your answers.

Start With What You Know

If the exam is parts-based, then I highly advise you to start with the parts where you are more comfortable and ones that you find more enjoyable. Not only will this ensure that you not waste time attempting trickier question but you will also feel more confident and optimistic knowing that you have already answered many questions correct. There is no strict rule governing where you need to start and finish your section-based exam so don't treat it in a strictly chronological order. Do what you feel happier doing first and leave the trickier bits for later.

Handwriting

Do you have handwriting that needs its own Rosetta Stone? If so, you need to make at least some effort to improve it or else you risk having your paper deciphered angrily and possibly downgraded. I highly suggest that when you are doing past papers in your revision, you start to focus also on the neatness of your handwriting. I personally haven't heard of any cases where a student's paper was simply illegible, but I am sure that they exist. If you find that your writing speed is significantly slower, then you might be better off not bothering with drastically improving your handwriting. If your teachers need to constantly remind you to write neater then please do pay attention. Nothing is more frustrating to an examiner then to decode your cluttered calligraphy.

Leaving Early

There are very few things in the world that frustrate and anger me more than seeing candidates get up and leave examinations with plenty of time to spare. You are given the time limit for a reason – use it! You must be incredibly careless to give up and just leave the exam with an hour to spare. There is absolutely no reason – none whatsoever – for you to leave before the time is up. Don't think you can just cross your arms on your desk and put your head down for a nap either. That would be equally retarded. I don't care whether you think you have answered all the questions and proofread enough. Unless you are 100% confident that you got 100% don't even consider leaving early. And no, you're not "cool" or "rebellious" for leaving with time to spare.

Proofreading

You absolutely must make sure you leave a few minutes at the end of your examination for proofreading. This is more important in non-essay based exams such as Mathematics and the Group 4 topics. Even in examinations for Economics, going back and making sure your diagrams are properly labelled could score you a few extra points. I'm not suggesting you make sure that you crossed all your T's and dotted all of your I's but at least make sure the majority of the exam is legible and that you avoided any silly mistakes. The few marks that you pick up when proofreading could prove vital if you're on the edge between two distinct marks. You will lose and gain most of your marks in the beginning and at the end of your examination – so make sure you make a positive start and always go back and proofread at the end.

Ignoring Distractions

Although the exams are supposed to happen in complete silence there may be times when distractions are simply inevitable. For example the kid sitting next to you who has never heard of cough medicine and is having non-stop bronchitis-like coughing. Or the student who accidently drops his pencil only for it to roll all the way across the room. I remember for one of my first Mathematics exams the weather in the morning was terrible. It was hailing, raining and thundering all at once. The fact that our examination centre had a semi-glass ceiling provided very surreal Dolby-Digital surround sound. It was probably the most frustrating thing to encounter when you are trying to focus on a HL Mathematics paper.

You need to teach yourself how to work around distractions. Don't become frustrated and punch the desk. Nor should you start to complain and lash out on your examination co-ordinator for having so many distractions. Just sit your exam and focus on what's in front of you. Do whatever you need to do to clear your head and relax. Perhaps invest and get used to wearing earplugs to drown out the noise?

Last Minute Exam Checklist

Have you done the following before entering your exam:

- Did you bring two pencils and two pens?
- Are they sharpened / refilled?
- Is your calculator charged?
- Do you have at least 1L of water for every 2 hours the exam goes for?

It may seem obvious, but last year when I did the exams I forgot some of these due to stress, and thus did not score as highly as I could have scored. Trust me, you'll want to have water when you're staring down a 20 mark multi-part physics question. The point is spare yourself the misery and just make sure you've prepared your stationary and water beforehand. However don't drink so much water that you have to take a bathroom break and waste valuable exam time – this is a mistake that too many students also make.

You will do fine.

Good luck with the exams!

24. Acing the Literature (Group 1) Exam

(contributed article)
The following sections of the book will attempt to cover in greater detail the specifics behind each IB group and subject. We begin with group 1: studies in language and literature.

Paper 1

This will be a short snippet on the best way to practice English and prepare for the exams, but first a short back story on my love hate relationship with the subject at hand. I was never particularly good at English. Despite trying very hard I always found it difficult to perform as well as other students, most of all I found it difficult to break that 6-7 barrier (which I did during the exams, but not with my external assessments). Had I known what I know now I would have been able to achieve a solid 7 without any problems. My class work averaged out to a 6, however to my astonishment I received solid 7s in both the exams (19/20 and 20/25). I was 3% off a 7, so had I put in that little extra effort to get my IA grade from a 13/20 to a 16/20 I would have been able to cross that grade boundary.

Now, the first step towards being good at English is of course listening and participating in class discussions, in addition to reading the books and texts that are assigned and doing your work on time. In addition to these tips a few things I found to be very useful were:

1)   To read around the subject, this entails learning about the authors, their style, their motivation and other authors that resemble them. By doing so you will be able to explore and reflect on very advanced concepts in your essays. You will be able to justify the author's choices in theme, rhetorical devices and why they even explored the

subject matter at hand. Put effort into this and you will be able to hit those top scores in the essays.

2)   Practice, practice, practice. Don't worry if your essays aren't perfect, as the exams approach, you should time yourself doing essays (past papers), get feedback from your teachers and improve using that feedback. The point is to improve one aspect of your writing each time, (these may include things such as organisation, inclusion of rhetoric devices, tone and so on). I was able to move from scoring 13/20 to a 19/20 in two months. You should aim to do at least five practice essays for each paper.

Paper 1 is a (comparative) textual analysis of one or two unseen texts. This section provides various ideas to develop the necessary skills for Paper 1. I have also provided a short list of tips, which should help you prepare for the exam in a more focused way.

The Band Descriptors

The first piece of crucial advice is something that you should do for all of your subjects really – get your hands on the official subject guide and read the band descriptors for the Paper 1. I'm not going to replicate them for fear of copyright infringement, but you know where to find this document. It will give you a sense of what the examiner is looking for and merely writing one relevant sentence which 'answers' one of the descriptors could easily get you an easy mark or two.

The Basics

Paper 1 asks students to comment on one of two texts within one and a half hours. Paper 1 asks students to compare and contrast one of two pairs of text within two hours. Passages for analysis may be complete pieces of writing or extracts from larger works. There is also the possibility of commenting on a visual text or an extract from a longer piece. Possible text types for analysis include:

advertisements, opinion columns, brochures, extracts from memoirs, or travel writing.

One of the texts from one of the pairs may be a literary text. Each individual text is presented with two guiding questions. HL students will not have guiding questions. Paper 1 counts for 25% of the final grade. It is assessed externally.

Firstly, whoever you are, wherever you live, whatever subjects you're taking, and whatever your favourite food might be, I want to let you know that you are capable of acing this.

You're capable of acing this because you're brave enough to be doing the hardest possible high school curriculum offered in the world. The technique that I'm about to outline was shown to me by my High School English teacher (she is awesome). It helped my peers and me a lot and I hope that it'll help you as well.

The P.E.A.L Method

I'm going to keep things short and simple because I know you're super busy. So, what is PEAL?

P = Point

E = Evidence

A = Analysis

L = Link

It's really simple and straightforward. Essentially, what we're trying to do here is to break down a seemingly complex and wordy text into a manner that we can best understand it and then effectively communicate it in our essay. Let me give you an example:

Imagine that you want to analyze the following paragraph:

'In LA, you can't do anything unless you drive. Now I can't do anything unless I drink. And the drink-drive combination, it really isn't possible out there.

If you so much as loosen your seatbelt or drop your ashes or pick your nose, then it's an Alcatraz autopsy with the questions asked later. Any indiscipline, you feel, any variation, and there's a bullhorn, a set of scope sights, and a coppered pig drawing a bead on your rug.

So what can a poor boy do? You come out of the hotel, the Vraimont. Over boiling Watts the downtown sky line carries a smear of God's green snot. You walk left, you walk right, you are a bank rat on a busy river. This restaurant serves no drink, this one serves no meat, this one serves no heterosexuals. You can get your chimp shampooed, you can get your dick tattooed, twenty-four hours, but can you get lunch?'

- Excerpt from Money by Martin Amis

It doesn't really matter where this comes from: in fact it'll be better if we don't know context here as you'll truly be able to see this technique put to good use. So, let's start.

(1) The point that I want to make here is that Amis (the author) utilizes hyperbole to effectively mirror the personality of the narrator (a man with a big ego called John Money) with the way the text is written.

(2) The Evidence that I'm going to use is:

'If you so much as loosen your seatbelt or drop you ashes or pick your nose, then it's an Alcatraz autopsy with the questions asked later.' to describe the danger of driving in LA.

and

'This restaurant serves no drink, this one serves no meat, this one serves no heterosexuals' to describe the varied and distinct tastes of the city.

(3) My Analysis is the following (in super rough terms, don't worry we're going to clean this all up when we put it all together):

Amis hints at his character's grandiose and outspoken personality by making him mention that seemingly small, inconsequential actions (picking one's nose, dropping a cig) can lead to huge car accidents, outlined in a humorous, entertaining way (Alcatraz autopsy with the questions asked later).

This use of hyperbole can also be seen when referring to LA's normally distinct and niche restaurants: Amis juxtaposes in a comical fashion the pickiness of these restaurants (this one serves no....etc) and can effectively communicate his character's distaste whilst simultaneously keeping in sync with his personality.

(4) Finally, you Link everything back to your thesis. I kind of already did this in my last paragraph by stating 'whilst simultaneously keeping in sync with his personality'. What you're trying to do here is to make sure that this micro-argument of yours is doing something to advance your thesis statement and makes cohesive, structural sense to your whole essay. As in this case we don't really have a thesis (I obviously can't write you a whole essay right now, but you get the point).

It can also be seen that (1) Amis utilizes hyperbole to effectively mirror the personality of his narrator (John Money) with the way in which the text is written. Indeed, (2) when describing the danger of driving in LA, Money states that 'If you so much as loosen your seatbelt or drop your ashes or pick your nose, then it's an Alcatraz autopsy with the questions asked later.' (3) Amis hints to his character's grandiose and outspoken personality by making him mention that seemingly small, inconsequential actions (picking one's nose, dropping a cig) can lead to huge car accidents, outlined in a humorous, entertaining way (Alcatraz autopsy with the questions asked later). This use of hyperbole can also be seen when referring to LA's normally distinct and niche restaurants: Amis juxtaposes in a comical fashion the pickiness of these restaurants (this one serves no) and is able to effectively communicate his character's distaste whilst simultaneously keeping in sync with his personality. (4) Insert Link Back to Thesis, something like: this all steers us towards the main idea that Amis is utilizing a wide variety of literary techniques to emphasize certain aspects of John Money's character to the reader.

This may seem like an extremely mechanical way of writing, but the transitions can get much more fluid, and you can intertwine your quotations in a nicer way than I just did to show you. This is just a basic, rudimentary way of writing: sometimes I hear my friends telling me that they get too lost reading the texts and can't structure their writing, and I advise this method to overcome that problem.

Prose or Poetry?

Many students find they enjoy doing the poetry for Paper 1 because it's easier to write about figurative language with poems and they are (usually) short, which gives more time for rereading and analysis compared to a two page extract from a novel. You will probably feel that you have a strength for either or, but if a passage speaks to you then go for that. It can be argued that with poetry, it is easier to make simple observations and add your own (somewhat dubious) connotations.

How Long to Plan?

Planning and annotating takes about 20 minutes depending on the difficulty of the piece. I would not recommend more than 25, otherwise you risk compromising the quality/quantity of your writing (but by the same token, consider it an investment in the quality of your work, so don't do it in 5 minutes).

Additional Tips

- Remember the big 5 (structure, stylistic devices, tone/mood, content/theme, audience/purpose)! Write about each of those and you're golden. Also remember to breath and take a break when the time is halfway. Just relax for a minute and set your mind straight. Read the texts multiple times and don't automatically settle for a text type you prefer because it might be that you would've had more to write about with the other text.

- Annotate what jumps off the page - recurrent ideas, devices, links in sentence structures or themes, punctuation... anything that holds a purpose (and the good thing about the poetry is everything is done for a reason). However, be sure to push these ideas further in your annotation than just noting them down - develop links, themes or motifs discussed by the author, negations in the text, tentative assumptions/conclusions and so on. This is by far the most important step and will save you time, brain space and stress once you begin writing.

The conclusion really brings home the analytical findings of your essay, hopefully in such a way so as to contribute to a nuanced discussion of the text. I would include sentences briefly (and I mean briefly!) recounting the findings of each paragraph, and then I would have a final closing sentence which summarized what I believ to be the author's/poet's main argument within the text. The conclusion often takes me 20+ minutes. I think strong control over language definitely helps here the most with a nice final clinching paragraph. Writing a conclusion is not something you just do after you've written your paragraphs with no planning in advance. Your paragraphs should all slightly hint towards it, and the conclusion should tie all the paragraphs together to strongly support your thesis statement.

Finally, try getting help from your teacher, or someone who you think could most closely emulate an examiner. Write an essay based on a practice prompt, either look at it yourself impartially or ask whenever you've found to look at it for you and point out its weaknesses. (While doing practice essays, I suggest limiting yourself to around 10-15 minutes less than exam time.)

Do that twice or thrice. Find out what mistakes are minor issues you can remember to handle, and what mistakes are major things you need to learn to do better.

Paper 2

The Paper 2 exam consists of six essay questions, only one of which must be answered during the timed period. The essay is to be written about the Part 3 literary texts. Therefore, it is a test of understanding literature in context. Although the questions will change from exam to exam, they will always focus on the connection between style, form, author, purpose and audience. Selecting good Part 3 texts is therefore essential.

These pages offer an overview of the requirements, the criteria and tips on Paper 2 essay writing. Besides familiarizing yourself with these pages, you will want to study previous exam questions, practice writing under exam conditions and research your literary texts carefully.

Although it seems as if a quarter of your IB grade is determined in one brief sitting, in fact you can do a lot to prepare for this exam so that it is not so nerve-racking. Careful planning and a clear strategy are half the battle. What one writes is only the tip of a very large iceberg.

The Basics

Answer 1 of 6 essay questions. SL and HL students receive exactly the same 6 questions.

Essay must answer one question in relation to both literary texts that were studied for Part 3.

Essay must answer one question in relation to 2 or 3 of the literary texts studied for Part 3.

Paper 2 grade counts for 25% of the final grade.

HOW TO STRUCTURE YOUR ESSAY:

A. Introductory paragraph
   a)   Motivator (address the question or statement)
   b)   Background summary (brief background to the texts and authors)
   c)   Thesis (what are you trying to prove?)
   d)   Focus (how will you prove your thesis? This is where you state your arguments)

B. Points (aka each body paragraph embodies this layout-aim for 3-4 paragraphs)
   a)   Point (topic sentence)
   b)   Evidence (quotation or description)
   c)   Analysis (specific focus on literary techniques)
   d)   Link (back to the topic in the question)

C. Concluding Paragraph
   a)   State Thesis (using different words/phrases)
   b)   Summary of main arguments (do not include new information)
   c)   Clincher (final sentence: should leave examiner satisfied you have covered all areas, but should also attempt to provoke further inquiry, or new dimension of looking at question)

So, this is the structure you want to follow. A common query that students have is in regards to how they should mention their quotes whilst writing their essays. What I like to do is integrate them fluidly within my paragraphs; this takes practice, but here are a few examples from my writing:

Natsume identifies intricacies and details in British culture that seem entirely foreign to him coming from Japan; he notes the impeccable fashion sense that surrounds him: *'herds of women walk around like horned lionesses with nets on their faces'* and notices a distinct height difference *'but when we rush past one another I see he is about two inches taller than me'* (Natsume in Phillips, R161). Natsume's experience as an outsider in Britain, according to Caryl Philips, *'helped him to become the fully mature and outstandingly gifted writer that he subsequently became'* (Phillips, R161).

I hope you can see what I'm trying to do; note that each quote naturally compliments the flow of the paragraph. You never need to explicitly state that you are about to use a quote; rather, just insert it within your body as nicely as you can.

The thesis statement of your essay is also extremely important; many English teachers have told me that often to gauge a writer's quality they examine his thesis statement. The more clear and compelling it is, the more credibility you gain as a writer in their eyes. Remember that you should be aiming to provide an argument; otherwise, your whole essay won't really have any meaning or substance (every single word you write should in some way back that thesis up).

BAD THESIS:
In this novel, Kanye West argues that we cannot justify the usage of drones and that their increased prevalence is harmful to members of society.

GOOD THESIS:

Though there may be considerable advantages to the usage of drones, West attempts to demonstrate that the worrying possibilities of mass surveillance and civilian losses, specifically in regards to the recent incidents in Orange County, are ultimately too precarious a path to follow.

I'm going to be honest: you should try to use flowery language to spice up your essays. It's just the truth. Before you go sit that exam, go on www.thesaurus.com and try to replace some common words you'd use with some nice, juicy ones.

In terms of transitioning between paragraphs aim to be clear and simple. 'It is possible to see the idea of..' or 'One argument put forward is...' are pretty good.

Now, listen up: I'm about to share a very valuable piece of advice with all of you:

Get your whole class to create a shared Google Doc with the following table:

Themes	Book A	Book B
	Quotes + Analysis	Quotes + Analysis

Then, together with your class, start filling the table.

It should get to a point where you have about twenty themes and plenty of quotes and analysis to back it up. Sharing is caring, and in this case, sharing will get you good grades.

Memorizing the quotes may seem daunting but it doesn't have to be that hard: what I recommend is that you paste about ten quotes you may use around your house. Literally post them outside your shower, perhaps, so that each time you bathe your beautiful body you also remember those quotes. Or put them up somewhere near your bed so that you go to sleep thinking about English.

25. IOC Tips and Tricks

(contributed article)
The Individual Oral Commentary is for many students one of the most daunting tasks during the IB. It involves an 8-minute oral commentary (much like Paper 1) on a poetry passage of approximately 30 lines, followed by questions regarding the same passage. Both SL and HL students must do an IOC. The difference being that HL students also need to engage in a 10 minute discussion with their teacher on one of two texts that they have studied in class. So, how can you prepare adequately for the IOC?

Oral Commentary Tips

Listen in class when analysing the poems. If you take detailed notes on the poems in class and ask questions to the teacher if there are any sections you do not understand or have neglected, this will make the final stages of your IOC preparation a lot easier. Listening to class discussions on the poems will also significantly reduce the chances of you getting to a specific part of a poem and having no prepared notes or analysis (not good if you get this extract in the final IOC).

It helps if you get a clean printed copy of each poem, with the poem at the center of the page and spaced out. This will enable you to make annotations in the margins (using a range of sources such as your class notes, your own interpretations, and the Internet). Make sure this is easy to read and revise from. By placing the poem at the centre of the page with annotations around it, you can have all the crucial information right in front of you.

You will need to revise these annotations enough until you can accurately reproduce them from memory. If you are given the same poem, you should be able to recall 90% of your scribbled annotations from memory by the time you go into your IOC. On IOC day, this will allow you to waste less time analysing the poem and considering techniques, and more time preparing and structing your oral response.

The Text Discussion

Make sure to read the text extract very carefully – and more than once. Reading the text extract at least twice will allow you to pick up on some of the complex issues that you miss in the first reading when you are focusing on plot and not broader themes and literary devices.

Also, you need to make sure to have a good set of notes. On average, you can have up to 20-30 handwritten pages of notes for the lengthier texts. Things such as plot analysis, structure, context, character analysis, thematic/symbol analysis should all be covered. This will give you a holistic and diverse understanding of the texts, and also give you option to link to all aspects of the text during the actual discussion.

Make sure to revise well from these notes. There is absolutely no point in spending many hours creating amazing notes if you don't understand them and remember them. You will need to make a conscious effort to revise each of the two texts at least five times before the final IOC. This way you will have a thorough understanding of the main conventions of the text, and will be able to recite certain quotes to support your answers.

It is also a good idea to practice an IOC discussion with a friend. Preferably you should run some trial IOCs in the week leading up to the real deal. You can do this in person or even on the phone. If you have a list of questions ready, this will be great practice. The questions don't have to be perfect – just enough to let your partner practice responding to oral prompts and displaying their knowledge of the text. You should benefit from this practise on both sides of the table. Doing it yourself will obviously show you your own flaws and let you know where you need improvement, but acting as the examiner can help you get in the mind of the examiner for when you do the real thing, so you're better able to know what sorts of things you should cover in your initial commentary, and how to respond to questions. It's all about practise.

General Tips

1) If you are studying poetry, you must know the poet's background, important themes/motifs, poetic concerns, and the general context behind the poem in question. Typically, these will all contribute to form a coherent introduction during which you would spend some time forecasting the thesis as well. How I usually organized my introductions was like this:
- Discuss title and author.
- Summarize the text briefly (at both the literal and subjective level, but the latter only slightly).
- Discuss background that is RELEVANT to the poem in question (for instance, for Sylvia Plath's "Two Sisters of Persephone", you would most likely have to refer to the explicit allusion to Greek mythology).
- Introduce the thesis (typically, I put the thesis at the end. The thesis should foreshadow your analysis and entry points).

2) If you are studying prose or plays, I suggest you literally re-read the book several times. I went to the extent of annotating each page of the novel and making important notes of motifs, dialogues, and important plot points for each chapter. Of course, this helps when the work is divided into chapters or sections, but if it isn't, you could always devise your own organization and structure to the work in question. If anything, this should only strengthen your understanding of the work. Given that you only really have a week to prepare, I suggest you first become very familiar with the text. Granted, you may get an excerpt from a novel

and not be able to immediately locate it. Even then, you still must try your best and contextualize.

3) Throughout your analysis, it is also quite important to embed both the larger effects of the features you are discussing. For instance, you could say: "the racist remarks and scathing diction are utilized to portray a shift in John's character". You could go about developing it and say this instead: "the racist remarks and scathing diction utilized by John aim to not only portray John being desensitized towards racism, but also the prevalence of Apartheid during 1950s." Not the best example, but it extends the analysis and indicates that you are knowledgeable about the topic.

4) In your conclusion, make sure to make some lasting impression. Don't be that person who says "In conclusion, poet X utilizes various literary devices such as Y and Z to develop her thesis". That's garbage. Rather, try to synthesize your analysis into a whole and give it a larger meaning. What does it all mean? What was Sylvia Plath's purpose in writing this essay? What other works of Plath does this work relate to? As a reader, what can we get away from it? Always remember that literature is a powerful tool. With just pen and paper, one person can evoke an emotional response from an entire population or spur change. Consider the larger implications of each work, even when you think there really isn't much -- I can assure you that it can be found.

5) Find out how your teacher intends to go about the IOC. Okay very technically speaking the rules: the IOC state that you should be presented with a series of envelopes each containing an extract totally unknown to you from any one of the texts/poems etc. you have studied. However, quite a large percentage of IB schools seem to implement alternative versions of the rules, including some where they will let you choose which texts they'll use and even the odd school where they let you choose your extract. Clearly if your teacher is going to let you select which novel you want to get, you're in with an advantage (and can save yourself

memorising the plot lines of 4 novels), so make sure you know how they want to play it and make the most of whatever you get.

6) Know the chronology of your texts. If your school hasn't let you choose the extract, you should find you have no idea what you're going to be given until you receive it. The good news is that your teachers are supposed to, according to the IB criteria, select an extract of significance within the novel. The bad news is that it's not always very obvious whereabouts in the novel this is, and you will be expected to put the extract into context. Consequently a reasonably large proportion of your preparation time should actually be dedicated to re-reading the whole text(s) and making sure you're quite clear about what events happen when. For some books this is easy, but for others with very skippy timelines (we all know the sort I mean) it's really hard, so make sure you put your effort into the right places!

7) Familiarise yourself with the author's style. An excellent way to prepare for your IOC is to familiarise yourself with the sorts of literary features and themes most common within a text. So, a good idea for your preparation is to flick through and look very closely at the author's styles for various things and make sure you're aware of a few key instances where the style is used. As an example (because I realise that's not the greatest explanation), Jane Austen always introduces characters with a few key descriptive words which cause the reader to form a view of a character usually before hearing them speak or seeing them do anything. So, knowing that this is one aspect of her style and that it's possible an introduction or description of a character might pop up in my IOC, I would make sure I was aware of at least one key instance of this happening so I could knowingly refer to it in my IOC.

Be sure to look at all aspects of writing style so you literally know enough about the general way the author writes that you can say something about almost any page in the book/poem etc.! You always want to show good knowledge of the novel/poems as a whole.

8) Use your preparation time wisely. You should be given 20 minutes to prepare for the exam and during this time it is imperative that you make the most of it. The number one thing is not to panic. Panic is wasting precious minutes. It's better to finish early and check your work than panic for 5 minutes and spend the next 15 writing frantically. Ideally, unless you're such a chilled person that you have no nerves, it's a good idea to have a plan of attack. I personally suggest the most simple which is to go through the extract line by line after reading through it once or twice.

The important thing is that you remember you probably only have enough time to make notes once, so the first notes you make will probably be the exact same ones you use 20 minutes later. There's no writing up into neat! Going through the extract underlining things is therefore not necessarily going to be that helpful if, once you're on the spot, you can't remember/read your own hand writing as to why exactly you underlined it. So, make sure that all the points you make are in a format which will be easy for you to understand in the actual thing. Also, although you only have a short period, as I mentioned before it's important to put things into context and match them up with other parts of the novel and other parts of the extract, so if you spot the same thing happening twice within your extract, link them up in such a way that you'll remember to mention both at once as you go through it. This makes your commentary seem a lot more structured than it otherwise would with only 20 minutes to prepare!

9) Imagine it is on paper and structure it. Literally imagine that your essay is being written by you rather than spoken by you. What do you need in every essay? Introduction, main body, conclusion. Don't forget to include an introduction (including that all-important putting the extract in context chronologically) and also a conclusion. I strongly suggest you

bullet point the contents of these rather than making them up on the spot because nerves can do terrible things when it comes to mind blanks, and the beginning and ending of presentations are both extremely important for the overall impact. You can do a great job but have a terrible ending and it's the lame ending which sticks in people's minds.

10) Don't fail to show outside knowledge! Reading through the extract and find yourself remembering a related fact/incident as you read? Say it! It's really important that you make the context (and your excellent knowledge of it) very clear, so if you remember something related, pop it in. Think that something a character does is reflective of something they do later, earlier, or their general behaviour? Mention the other event as well. Don't waste loads of time on it, keep all these outside points reasonably succinct, but whatever you do don't overlook them or fail to mention them.

11) Set yourself up to achieve fluency via knowing how you work. Just like with the IOP, you want to appear extremely competent and fluent. Generally, when in a state of panic, the only way to achieve this (besides obviously making sure you know what you're talking about!) is to make excellent notes so when panic strikes, you can stay on track. I'd strongly suggest you practice going through an extract that you pick at random and making notes on it prior to the actual thing. Then try imagining what you'd say based on the notes you've made yourself after 20 minutes. If the notes you've made aren't enough to stop you blanking, re-consider the way in which you make notes.

12) Final tip. Know EVERY literary device by heart. Not just the generic ones like metaphor, simile, allusion, etc. Know the obscure ones like asyndeton, synecdoche, antithesis, etc. Don't forget that syntactical analysis is also important, especially for prose. It helps when you know grammar too (infinitive verbs, cataloguing, etc.).

26. Blasting Through Language B

(contributed article)

Language B is a great opportunity to score a 6 or 7 easily for most students. For convenience and consistency, this section is written from the point of view of someone taking French as their Language B subject, however almost all the advice can be applied to other languages as well.

The key to doing well in IB Language B is be open minded and willing to do the work set by the teacher. This subject can be an easy 7 or 6 if you put in the effort and do all the assignments set. This is how I was able to attain a 7 in French, by not skipping on homework. Furthermore, it is important to use what you learn in class in public. To accomplish this it may be in your interest to get a language tutor or if you live in a francophone country, take a step outside and join some sports clubs in order to meet and socialise with locals. If you are a shy person this may be very difficult to do, so having a French tutor is the best option. By having one hour of extra French practice will help you to develop your vocabulary.

In addition to practice and doing homework, maximize your grades on the internal assessments like the Tache Ecrite and the oral recording. Meet with your teacher and get corrections and advice on how to improve both assessments. This should allow you to achieve higher grades even if you do not reach your true potential in the exam. Having a French tutor will help with the Tache Ecrite and socialising outside of class in French will help with the oral. Follow these steps and you will most certainly achieve a high grade in French B SL.

The written task is something that you have complete control over. Don't procrastinate, get advice early from your teacher, and then keep working on it for a good two weeks. What you can also do is actually show your copy of the written task to other French teachers in your school; this is not cheating the system as the IB clearly states your professor can only give you feedback once. But what about other consenting professionals in the school? After all, you're just attempting to give in your best possible work. In the long run, it'll pay off.

I got a 7 in French B, and a lot of my peers did very well in their respective Ab-initio classes as well. Even if you feel that you don't understand French or Spanish (or whatever language you're taking), the key to doing well in such case is to just understand enough so that you can nail the reading comprehension Paper 1. I'm serious; Paper 1 should be maximum points for a lot of you.

Getting a 7 in IB French SL isn't as impossible as it might seem. Admittedly, French B (even at SL) in the IB can be a challenging and daunting course if you are not 1) fluent/native or 2) been on a long enough exchange that you are comfortable with your French (even if just speaking) or 3. a language wiz that is just naturally good at languages. However, it is still possible to get a 7 in this subject if you are none of the above (me). It does require quite a bit of effort, but the work pays off if you stick to it.

Read, read, read, read, read. Yes, read. Find articles online relating to the topics you are studying in class and draw out all the specific vocab and phrases that could be useful in writing tasks or that may pop up in Paper 1s. You can compile vocabulary lists for Core topics (because these only come up in Paper 1s) and compile notes for Option topics (so you have phrases to memorise for Paper 2). Notes are literally just a ton of phrases bullet pointed in a word document, under subheadings to sort out the "subtopics" of each topic. A very easy way to "study" for French, especially as it is quite brainless – all you must do is type up all the phrases that you like/ have highlighted!

Memorise those phrases for your Paper 2s. Generally, you will study 2 options for your Paper 2, so if you learn as many good subject-specific phrases for each you have 50% of your Paper 2 down. Add that to the vocab that you have compiled and it makes it 70%.

Learn your grammar structures. A good Paper 2 does not need to be overly complicated, it just must be accurate. "Sophisticated" language structures could just be the subjunctive used correctly and in the right place, or the correct use of a direct object pronoun. Especially at SL, they are more concerned with your accuracy. That's 90% of your Paper 2.

Learn your text types. It's five easy marks that you should always be getting. Practice a wide variety of text types so that you are free to choose whatever question no matter the text type in the final exam. Be comfortable with your question form for interviews, and with imperatives in brochures. Know how to structure a formal and informal letter, an article and a diary entry. You'll always have a favourite, but you still need to practice – what if your favourite text type is paired with your least favourite question in the final exam?

Practice good exam technique for your Paper 1. For example, if a verb is being used in the question, there should be a verb somewhere in your answer (if the question is asking for a phrase that is synonymous with "concerne chacun" then your response should have "verb —"). Learn how to manage your time and get used to the amount of time (roughly) you should be spending on each article so you finish in time to do a good check. Paper 1 can be very challenging at first when you haven't learned your grammar structures and vocabulary, but once you start reading more, writing more and just doing more French. Paper 1 is a source of easy marks that can boost your grades.

Practice speaking French often. Participate in class, find a friend you can do French debates with once a week, get a speaking tutor. There are so many ways to get yourself more exposed to the language and more confident speaking it. This will help your interactive orals massively! As for the individual oral, practice describing photos related to the option topic you are studying at home by yourself and then practice linking it back to the topic to complete your presentation. It is useful to learn phrases that will help you describe different elements of the photo and linking phrases you can use to round out your presentation. Subject specific phrases are great for when your teacher asks you questions on the topic, so learn them, and also know very clearly what your opinion is on that topic, because the IB loves it when you have an opinion.

Complete your written assignment to the maximum of your potential. Your teacher should provide plenty of guidance with this, so it is a source of relatively easy marks as it is weighted 20%. Find good articles on a core topic you are comfortable with and stick to the text type that you know best. Heed your teacher's advice and do a thorough proofread before you submit your final copy.

Acing the Oral

The French Individual Oral can be scary. For me, it came 2nd on my list of scariest IAs. But never fear, because even if you have never been on a language exchange trip, do not like your language B and just do not have a knack for languages, you can still do well in this internal assessment, I promise. (But you still have to work hard for it). Here are my 7 tips on effective preparation and study for the oral:

1. Have your notes compiled, or if you haven't already, start now.
2. Memorise the key phrases, relevant to the topic that you are studying. We call this subject specific vocabulary. The more you have of this, the better. All of this will help you immensely in your discussion.

3. Link words and phrases are essential. You need to be able to effectively link between the photo and the topic to show the examiner your knowledge of the issue at hand. Photo-describing phrases. Obvious now you think about it, right?

4. Grammar! Nothing worse than making a load of grammar errors in the oral- sure-fire way to lose marks. Make sure you have revised your grammar, and that you understand and can execute the structures accurately. Simple things like masculine and feminine nouns (especially the ones that come up over and over) must be perfect!!

5. Practice, practice, practice describing photos and linking them back to the topic. Find photos on the web and practice them and record yourself. You can request practice runs with your teacher, or just practice with friends or your tutor. There really isn't anything more useful than this..

6. Participate in class. Sounds irrelevant, but when you begin to get involved in class discussion you'll find it is a lot easier to answer the questions in the discussion. Also very useful to have those discussions with friends and classmates.

7. Stay calm and relaxed. Try not to think too much about it, and if need be, don't talk about it with friends. While you are waiting outside the room the most important thing is to stay calm and perhaps go over some of the key phrases in your head. Speak clearly, and if you need to fill gaps try "euuuuu" instead of "um" (it really breaks the flow).

Anticipated Subject

We covered anticipated subjects in the first few chapters of this guide. Language B is an excellent choice for finishing an IB subject in your first year, I have seen plenty of students do so and do so successfully. You should really inquire with your IB coordinator and language teachers if this is a possibility. It will save you the hassle of studying for 6 subjects in your final exam stretch, and you could already possibly have a grade 7 in the bag.

27.The Group 3 Struggle

(contributed articles)

The Social Sciences can be some of the hardest subjects to study for as they require one to retain lots of information, whilst at the same time necessitating critical evaluation. With Economics for example6 to get the top mark, you need to know your diagrams by heart, as well as all the definitions. No way around that.

However, what separates the students that get 6s from those that get 7s is the evaluation. Examiners want to see an opinion; they want to see that you can weigh the pros and cons of an issue, and then decide, based on evidence and case studies, what the 'right' option is. This not only applies to Economics, but all the other social sciences as well. Here, we've examined a few students that each got 7s in their respective Group 3 subjects, and how they did it.

Economics

This can't be stressed enough: do actual exam questions. If you can get in the habit of answering essay long questions at least once every week in your group 3 subject, you will have a huge advantage over individuals that do not do this. This improves your evaluation skills, allows you to distinguish between different keywords in questions (for example: evaluate, describe, analyse, compare), and ensures that come exam time, you won't be fazed by something unusual.

I would also recommend reading the news on a daily basis. Real-life examples are like gold dust when writing for 15 mark evaluative essays. Besides, reading the news will ensure that you have a grip on what's going on in the real world, outside of the IB. Out of all the group 3s that you could choose to take in the IB, I would have to say that Economics is one of the easiest. Getting a 7 in this subject is not hard at all, just follow 3 simple rules:

Practice Essay writing – dig out past papers and write those essays/data responses under timed conditions, and then give it to your teacher to mark. Slowly, you will find your pitfalls are in the same places (for me, it was forgetting to define!) and eventually these mistakes can be easily fixed.

Understand your content – so much in Economics doesn't necessarily need to be rote learned, but you do need a solid understanding of each topic and how it relates to the other topics to write those essays well.

Write syllabus notes – write yourself a set of notes under the syllabus bullet points. Try to summarise as much as you can so it's easier to learn, and in doing so, you will find that you understand the content a lot better! You can also draw mind maps to help sort out all the connections between the different topics. Try to write your notes as you go along, the IB Economics syllabus is lengthy and you will have a hard time trying to finish them all right before the exams.

For complete information on how to ace your economics IAs, we strongly suggest getting our book devoted to just that: *The IB Economics Commentary: Examples and Advice* by Alexander Zouev (available on Amazon).

Geography

For Geography, Paper 1 is very easy if you have studied. Thus, it's important to maximize your marks on this paper. Apart from memorizing a few case studies and knowing your definitions (which is a given, at this stage), there are only graphs and diagrams to analyse.

For this, I recommend the 'OSO' Easy technique. Essentially, you say something that is Obvious about the graph, something that is Specific (quote a numerical datapoint), and something that is Odd. This will almost guarantee you all the marks for that question.

I also advise studying hard for Paper 3, the part of the course that encompasses Global Interactions. This is a section of the course that a lot of students are often intimidated by. If you can learn all the definitions and engage actively in class with your teacher, this paper essentially looks at your ability to recall information.

Paper 2 is more of a lottery. Some options are easy, some are really tough. I personally found the Tourism option to be very easy, and actually self-studied it in two days before the exam (this is by no means a recommendation for your approach however). I got a solid 6, and thus for my limited studying time, was happy. With it you can maximize your Paper 1 and Paper 3 in Geography, Paper 2 shouldn't be too much of an issue.

The IA is something that you just must work hard on. Don't leave it to the last minute, as examiners will see that you've put in minimal effort. Instead, gain feedback from your teacher and ask them how you can improve. Ask your peers, and help each other. To be completely honest, the Geography IA is normally not a big concern for IB students, and thus as long as you are well-planned and don't panic, you'll be just fine.

Try "profiling" countries that you use for case studies. For example, I profiled China because China is often a country that many of my case studies overlap (One Child Policy, globalisation, disposal of wastes, etc.) and made several statistics on it like population, GNI, migration, etc. I'm doing this for all my countries that are very relevant. It can be helpful in getting a clear idea if anything comes up. Also helps with memorizing (for me, you may be different).

Memorize case studies, know them off the top of your head. Know how to spell them right, for example the Kissimmee

River. Be sure that you can write a good paragraph about each of them, and for higher marks memorize specific numbers: dates, statistics, places, etc.

Another tip is that Paper 1 essay question essentially covers three of the four core topics. You could essentially study essay topics for two of the four topics and 1 question that you studied should come up in the Paper 1. I've been doing this method for IB1 & IB2 mock exams and it all worked out fine. But if you're a "better safe then sorry" you can always learn three topics essays and omit the topic you hate the most.

Try to learn flexible diagrams to draw for essay questions. For example, population pyramids are good go-to for many of the core points like Development or Populations in Transition, and even migration (for example, you could draw the Philippines and have a huge gap and label that as "OFW (Oversea Family Worker)" which can link to P3 Globalisation too!). Diagrams really add to the last criterion of the mark-scheme.

Prepare your hand for a lot of writing. Practice writing essays under a time limit. Remember Paper 2 and 3 are on the same day normally, that's pretty much four essays in a row. Set your timer, take out a pencil, and gets lots of practice beforehand working against the clock.

History

Essay structure in history matters just as much as actual knowledge. You can know absolutely everything but if you can't communicate it in a way that is cogent and clear, you won't get high marks. For Paper 1, you should become a sort of 'wizard' at analysing all kinds of sources. To do this, you should study a lot of past papers and improve your information collecting skills.

For Paper 2, outlining your essay is just as important as writing it. Thus, I recommend spending about 5 minutes before you start writing your essays on making a clear outline of what you're actually going to write. Don't forget that history isn't just about memorizing a whole lot of events in a particular order. You have to learn to think critically, and analyze all the aspects of an event; its causes, implications, consequences, motives etc.

For complete information on how to get a grade 7 for your IB History, we strongly recommend getting our book *How to Write an IB History Essay: The Safe Hands Approach* by Joe Thomas (available on Amazon)

Business and Management

It's a known fact that only 4% of all IB BM students worldwide achieve a grade 7. This is one of the hardest courses to earn a 7 – but if you get there, you will breeze past any first year university-level business program. That being said, ask your teacher for a command term sheet and the rubric/marking criteria for answers. Failing that, ibbusinessandmanagement.com has a great command sheet that breaks down all of IB's favourite command terms (comment, identify, analyse, to what extent, evaluate, etc.) what each term expects, and the general order of marks allocated to each command term.

Get as much material as you can from your teacher and ask to see the syllabus guide. There is also a very complete Internal Assessment guide that breaks down the criteria and how to structure it. Get your hands on that too. The more information you have at your disposal, the higher your chances of a good grade. Also, you have to think outside of what you learn in class for a 7, so read up on business articles and get used to using 'business language'/terminology.

Solving past papers will be good as far as practicing how you structure your answers according to the marking criteria. It's an opportunity to get used to IB answer structure, and your ability to form arguments and back them up. But do it sparingly, it may not be the best use of your time in Year 1, as you'll have to focus primarily on understanding the main content and concepts.

You can grade your own work, which will be handy for the IA as well. Read your paper and compare it to the mark scheme, look at what you've missed out. For example, is it too focused on explanation of facts/figures and not enough on analysis or recommendation? Same applies for past papers and sheet-work that your teacher gives you. It's also worth buddying up with your classmates and taking a free period to check each other's class work to see what went wrong and what went right.

28. Beating Biology

(contributed article)

The sciences are fundamentally different and it is this difference that makes one more difficult than the other. Biology is a game of memorisation; if you can remember everything then you are guaranteed a 7 as the critical thinking involved is minimal when compared to the other sciences. Nonetheless, it is extremely easy to lose marks for missing out on simple points, so practice a lot with the question bank and past papers and understand what the question is asking.

How to Guarantee a 7 in Bio

Here are a few tips that got me through HL Bio and might help you too.

As you may know Biology is a very content-heavy subject, but there are no complex concepts that you need to understand. It is just pure memorisation but there are some techniques that can make the HL bio trip less stressful and more enjoyable.

It is important that you make NEAT notes that are aesthetically pleasing. This may sound obvious but if your notes are visually appealing, you will have a better time looking at them. The more often you look at them, the better. As you go through the topics try to summarise all the information on a single A4 sheet. Condensing information will make you memorize more effectively. It is also crucial that you go over the topics more than once and you should make various different note sheets per topic as you move through the syllabus. You should never exactly copy the book.

Use different styles of study methods. It is important that you don't only stick to flashcards but also make yourself big summary sheets. Use drawings, colours, neat handwriting…

Try and be as diverse as possible in order to transform the information from the book into something that is your own. This will really help process and remember all the information. Bio is also one of those subjects where if you have a friend who just makes really neat and awesome notes, you should try to get a copy from them if you can.

It's crucial that you familiarise yourself with the exam structure and style. I recommend getting the Questionbank even if there is a new syllabus. The more questions you do, the better. This is really important for the big 20 mark questions. Reading the questions and looking at the markschemes helps you understand how the examiners think. It is also imperative that you go through your answers using the markschemes after a biology test. The more you do this the better you will get at writing answers that are tailored to the question asked. Basically just try and do as many past papers as possible; it really does help.

Study from markschemes (for the 20 mark questions). Some questions like "explain the process of translation or transcription" just never change and are recycled every other year. I recommend doing this for a few big questions per topic so you can be sure that one will come up at least. However, this should be done close to the exam time.

Keep your notes on display in your room or bathroom. The more often you see your notes the better. Even if it's just 3 minutes while you are brushing your teeth. This is really important for diagrams as there are around 30 of them that you must memorize.

The best way to do well on your exams is to know the material, so lots of revision. Most importantly is to find a way that works for you. I personally find that re-writing notes to make them look more appealing works best for me. The other important part is being consistent, even if it's only twenty minutes a day it really helps to keep material fresh in your mind. The final piece of advice, given to me by my coordinators, is to try to make connections between topics and between subjects. So for instance in both Chem and Bio you do an organic chemistry unit, you can try to overlap knowledge there.

You need to know that there are three types of examination questions:

1) Multiple Choice Questions (Paper 1): You choose the answer from four possible choices. Read them all, eliminate any answers to narrow them down. Always give answers and never leave questions empty. Leave the hard ones till the end and focus on the straightforward ones.

2) Structured Questions (Paper 2 and 3): Each question is broken down into sections. Answers are written in spaces or on lines. If you run out of space, complete elsewhere on the examination sheet itself, but clearly indicate where you wrote the rest of the answer. In paper 3, you are allowed to have extra paper. The marks are allotted at the end of each question; useful for you to know how many points and details to include in the answers. An example of this type of question is the data-analysis question (beginning of paper 2). It requires you to analyze graphs and compare results. (See Data-Analysis Questions).

3) Free Response Questions (Paper 2): These questions require long and detailed answers on lined paper. You are the boss of the style of answer (best choice, tables, carefully annotated diagrams..). Usually the questions will direct you. Sometimes (Section B) you are given choices. Read them carefully to choose the question that best suits you and you know you can answer the best. Always follow a logical sequence in arranging your answer and avoid irrelevant information. Try to make your handwriting as legible as possible.

Basically, 50% of the questions require factual recall. So recharge your memory! These questions require direct answers: LIST, STATE, OUTLINE or DESCRIBE. The other 50% involves expressing ideas that are more complex or involve using your knowledge of things you haven't been taught.

These questions usually start with:

EXPLAIN - Sometimes it involves giving the mechanism behind things with a logical chain of events. It is a 'how' sort of explanation with 'therefore' being the keyword. However, sometimes it involves giving reasons or causes; a 'why' sort of explanation with 'because' being the keyword.
DISCUSS - Sometimes, you have to include arguments for and against something. Try to give a balanced account. Sometimes, you might include a series of hypotheses without making a final choice.
SUGGEST - Mostly never taught. Use your overall biological understanding to find answers. As long as they are possible, they will receive a mark!
COMPARE - refer to previous section to see a detailed explanation.
DISTINGUISH - Include only the differences in your answer. Use 'whereas' to help.
EVALUATE - Assess the value, importance or effect of something. How useful is the technique/model? What are its impacts on others/environment? Use your own judgment and criticism as long as it's valid and biologically correct.
Other action verbs are more straightforward and you'll probably answer them easily.

Data-Analysis Questions

I know many of us suffer from these types of questions. Read the question carefully. Underline any keywords in the question (sometimes, there are hidden facts that examiners put to see if you pay attention or not). Always underline action verbs in the questions (discussed above). This helps in case you forget or get messed up.

Start with the question, see how many marks are allotted and solve accordingly (2 marks means at least 2 major points in the answer, and so on). In case of graphs, always read the title of the graph, each axis and its units. In case of calculations, show your working and always indicate the units.

Study the data presented carefully many times (but watch out for the time). Be familiar with it and start solving. Practice such questions in your free time. They might really be annoying, but it really helps in the long run.

Resources

I would suggest revising from a range of different sources - I prefer using Bioninja (http://ib.bioninja.com.au) and other online IB Biology websites to make notes from since the textbooks either have too much or too little of certain bits of the syllabus. If your teacher isn't great or you're just not able to concentrate in class, check out Alex Lee on Youtube – this channel basically got me through Bio HL. I-Biology.net is another holy grail of IB Biology resources.

To be perfectly honest, there is such a myriad of resources out there that you just need to spend a good couple of hours searching around and finding what you find works best for you. The official IB Biology study guides are also great, but you should make sure that your revision is always remaining active and not just reading/glossing over.

29. Cracking Chemistry

(contributed article)
Chemistry is halfway between Biology and Physics. It combines large amounts of memorization with elements of critical thinking and analysis. What this means is that even if you know your theory inside out you will still struggle when it comes to certain complex problems, more so than in biology. I also suggest you use past papers and the Questionbank extensively to help you review chemistry.

Chemistry is one of those subjects that at first glance is extremely difficult, this is due to the fact that there is so much new content introduced. The amount of "stuff" you have to know is significantly larger in IB chemistry than in any pre-IB course. Concepts such as orbitals, quantum chemistry and modern analytic chemistry are completely new and might be difficult to understand at first, especially with such an interlinked subject as Chemistry. This means that you will need concepts you still haven't studied to understand those you are currently studying. It might be especially difficult for those of you who like to understand the fundamentals of principles (as I do), as you still haven't studied those principles.

There are a few ways to solve this issue and improve your understanding of chemistry. Firstly (the least suggested method), would be to simply memorize all that you are taught and hope that once you have gone over most of the subject things will start to come together (they usually do, however you will need to go over certain concepts). The alternative is to go above and beyond the scope of the course. This means reading ahead in your book and discussing what you have learned with your teacher to understand the basics and fundamentals and linking ideas together.

Once you are able to link concepts together (which usually happens by the start of the second year of IB chemistry), the subject becomes much easier. Don't take this as an excuse to not work during the first year, as a matter of fact you should put a lot of energy during the first year to gain a very solid grasp of the basics which will allow you to understand and perform better with more difficult concepts.

As always I suggest you download the Questionbank to practice what you have learned. Despite the change in course, the question bank is still very useful and I suggest that you start using it 3 to 4 days before any test. Go through all the questions and understand the concepts. When it comes to chemistry there is no better way to study than to take quick notes while reading and answering Questionbank problems at the end of each chapter/topic.

Look through the specification, there are some points that you actually need to rote learn as an example (like the medical uses of some isotopes). I can't stress this one enough. When you revise, look through the specifics and ask yourself if you understand every point. My teacher missed a load of spec points so I used Richard Thornley to learn them (check the YouTube channel, it is a lifesaver).

If you're good at rote learning / memorization, or have the time to do so, I strongly recommend learning all of organic chemistry. It's a heavy rote learning topic but if it comes up in the exam you can easily get full marks on any organic chemistry question since you don't actually need to apply many, if any, concepts at all.

Learn how to do the calculations. The Henderson-Hasselbach equation is very useful for the acids section, but it isn't on the specification. I recommend learning that equation off by heart, because I've seen some 4 mark questions where you can simply plug the numbers into the HH equation (there's a longer way to do it too if you're wondering why they're 4 marks)

30. Figuring Out Physics

(contributed article)
Physics might be a subject which requires relatively less memorization; however, the concepts explored are multidimensional and the critical thinking required is advanced. You might be asked to prove things using formulas, or derive certain formulas, or explain unknown concepts through previously studied ones. It is natural that you use the Questionbank and past papers to supplement your studying. After completing a chapter in each topic, do a few questions, reflect and then continue with the next chapter. I suggest this technique with all the sciences but especially with physics.

To show the importance of practice I will bring up Pablo and use him as an example. He is a smart guy who got into Oxford, but if it wasn't for the 7 he received in HL physics he wouldn't have made it. He was predicted a 7 in History and Economics, however to his astonishment he didn't get them, yet his practice and hard work for physics paid off in the form of a 7. A few weeks before the exams Pablo would come to my house on Fridays (desperate times require desperate measures, such as not partying on Fridays) and we would get to work. There really isn't any way around it. I had always been rather good at the sciences so Pablo used me as a resource (don't worry I don't feel exploited). He would practice Question bank problems and if he ever encountered any issues he would ask for some help. I helped him where I could (this helped me solidify my own understanding) and where I couldn't help him I went and did the research (this helped me spot some gaps in my learning). We did this for a few weeks until he felt confident with his physics and both of us came out on top.

This example was meant to emphasize two points: firstly that there is no way around studying, and secondly that you should work with your friends when needed (two minds are better than one).

It's important to know what the question is asking of you, more specifically how much information you should include when extrapolating the age of the universe from the Hubble constant or how many data points you should test to determine whether the correlation of the graph is correct. To get good at this you should take a look at the science command terms. This can be achieved as easily as Googling "chemistry/biology/physics IB command terms". (Command terms apply to all subjects and I suggest you understand all the pertinent ones).

Be greedy, it's the IB and you need to snatch points wherever you can (this idea applies to all the subjects). In the sciences the best way to do this is to place particular attention to the internal assessments and paper 2 of the exams. If you put in the correct amount of attention into the IAs you can score upward of 90% (this sounds high, but remember use all the resources at your disposition: teachers, friends, and the Internet). You should also get better at doing Paper 2's, as they bring you the largest chunk of the final grade (36%). This entails learning the command terms, getting good at structuring answers and time management. It also means picking up the book and learning thoroughly the data analysis techniques that will be asked of you in the first part of the paper. If you can accumulate points in these 2 parts (IA and Paper 2) then you are guaranteed a passing grade and achieving that 7 will be even easier.

Revision Examples

The following test advice doesn't only apply to the sciences but all subjects you will do in the IB. Memory retention techniques at their core are very similar, so listen carefully to the advice below and extrapolate as much as you can.

Reading is never enough to memorize or understand a concept (unless you are a genius, and I'm guessing you aren't), you need to take that information and reformulate it and apply it. The more (and more often) processing your brain does of the information the better you will retain it. That's why learning is so dynamic.

Reading is not enough on its own. To ensure a full understanding, you have to take notes, scribble on the page, highlight and connect concepts you read about. I annotate things, draw arrows that link ideas and solve problems. I also fill in the blanks or steps that might have been skipped by the book in proving formulas. The point is to transfer your thinking process onto the page.

Taking notes is extremely important. However, copying the book isn't enough. You must add an extra level of processing to the copying. This may include rephrasing what you have read, underlining key words, creating your own examples, drawing diagrams or explaining to yourself concepts that you didn't understand before.

I invest time and energy into my notes, so that I may refer to them in the future when I have forgotten the topic and actually understand them. Evidently this is a time-consuming process, so be smart; prioritize subjects based on how much difficulty you have retaining concepts, how technical it is, etc.

Don't forget to pair your note taking with sessions of question answering (this is the most important step, never skip it). However before the exams (a few days) I suggest that you go over your notes, questions you did in the past and found difficult as well as all the material provided in the exams (data booklets and so on). Annotate your data booklet and make sure that you understand everything in it.

A trick I learned before the exams is that not all the useful formulas are included in the data booklets (this is more evident for chemistry that physics).

31. The Group 4 Project

(contributed article)

The idea here is actually pretty simple: students are basically just split up into groups with representatives from at least two sciences and told to design, perform, and make a presentation on an experiment based on a given theme They're basically grading you on teamwork and how well everyone in the group understands the experiment and the concepts behind it, rather than the experiment design, outcomes, or anything like that. Ours was actually pretty enjoyable. As long as you work well with your group mates, everything should be fine.

The group 4 project is a piece of work that all IB students have to do – it is so important for you to do this, that you fail the Diploma if you do not do it (but it doesn't technically count towards anything...) As such, your school should be making you aware of this.

For those that do not know, the project is unusual in that, the process you go through is far more important than the actual outcome. The idea is that you work with other students in a multidisciplinary way. This may sound a little strange so I would explain it in the following way: there are 3 phases to the project ...

1. The Planning Phase.

The aim of this stage is for each small group of students (approx 6) to come up with a suggestion for the Global Title of the G4 Project. The students in the Planning teams should cover the G4 subjects at the school wherever possible.

It is important that each and every person MUST contribute to this process. It is everyone's responsibility to consider what their subject could contribute to the suggested Titles. For example, there is no point suggesting a title if you can't think what the Physics students could do with it. In most schools, the G4 subjects are Bio, Chem, Phys, EVS, DT.

Examples of possible titles are:

Concrete

Biology: medical effects of dust

Chemistry: purity of limestone, additives, chemical attack, the setting process

Design Technology: composites, choice of material, reinforcement

Environmental Systems: impact of extracting and using sand, cement, aggregate

Physics: strength, composite theory, thermal properties

Analysis of local and/or traditional building materials

Biology: effect of removal on local environment, support of growth of organisms e.g. insects

Chemistry: acid rain, salinity, combustibility

Physics: mechanics, stress, heat transfer, ventilation, insulation

Effect of caffeine of physical performance

Biology: effect on respiration, blood pressure, heart rate, reflex time and   balance

Chemistry: sources and composition of caffeine, determining caffeine levels in these sources

Physics: measuring power output (stair climbing, cycles, speed rotations)

Ski project

Biology: skeletal structure, muscles, temperature loss, anthropometrics

Chemistry: snow quality, artificial snow, waxes, materials

Design Technology: buildings, materials

Environmental Systems: forest destruction, erosion, economic impact

Physics: aerodynamics, friction, gravity, structure, heat loss, insulation

Science in the theatre

Biology: reducing stress for performers

Chemistry: creating safe special effects

Design Technology: designing new sets, lighting

Environmental Systems: improving air quality

Physics: creating new lighting effects

Factors influencing performance in a 400m race

Biology: heart beat, biorhythms, sleep, fatigue, stress

Chemistry: isotonic drinks and diet

Design Technology: design and materials for track, shoes, sports drinks containers

Physics: elasticity, shock absorbance, wind, temperature

2. The Action Phase.

Usually students are put into small groups (approx 3-4) to do the actual work. You will do a short piece of research as a team. You need to split the work up and every member of the team must take responsibility for this part.

It is vital to remember that the actual outcome is not important, it is the fact that the students actually worked together and made something happen.

3. The Reporting Phase.

This is where the school asks you to normally give a presentation to explain what you did and asks questions for a few minutes at the end.

Final Comments:

The one BIG piece of advice about the Group 4 Project is to enjoy it – do not try to avoid it or do nothing. Work hard because these strange moments do not happen that often. Enjoy the work and engage with what you are doing – it should then be fun and you should get excellent marks for it. Also keep it mind that it counts for **0%** of your overall grade (you just need to 'pass it') so don't sweat it too much.

32. Mastering HL Maths

(contributed article)

The advice in this chapter is written primarily with HL Maths in mind – however almost all of it is still applicable to Studies and SL.

There is simply no way around it; you have to study and practice. Knowing the theory isn't good enough, especially when you are doing HL Maths. Throughout the two years of mathematics I was consistently scoring between 4s and 5s on my tests, and even scored a shaming 28% on paper 1 in the mock exams. It goes without saying I thought I was going to fail the IB, however I used this stress and panic to my advantage. I began very intensive studying and in a period of 3 months was able to clock in around 120 hours of math studying; that amounts to about an hour and a half of math each day, thanks to which I scored a solid 6 in my exams.

I organised my math studying as follows:

I used the Cambridge IB Mathematics HL book, and did most of the problems from there (even the easy and repetitive ones, as these teach you small tricks). I also spent some extra time doing the more complicated problems and didn't give up too soon. This book allowed me to really learn all the tricks that you will need for solving impossible IB problems. I strongly suggest you purchase this book and use it as a primary source of practice.

Upon finishing each chapter, I would turn to the QuestionBank and create a mini test with relevant questions. You have to get used to the IB formatting and understanding how they might attempt to trick you (initially I could honestly only understand one in three questions but by the end I could understand every one. This however didn't mean that I could solve all of them). You should also understand how the mark scheme works, because if you do not show your workings you could lose marks even though your answer is correct. Finally your teachers usually give you questions from the QuestionBank, so if you are lucky some you have done might come up again (this always helps with the predicted grade). Any questions I didn't understand I would bookmark and ask my math tutor or class teacher for help. (I had a tutor all year round; I strongly suggest this if you can afford it).

Finally, attempt all the questions in the exam, even if you only know the first half of the problem still attempt to solve it. The IB mark scheme works in mysterious ways and you can always get a few points here and there. These points might be the difference between a 5 and 6 or 6 and 7.

54%. When your teachers said you are capable of taking Higher Level Mathematics, they never explained that it meant dropping from a "straight 7s" student to barely getting half the marks on a test. It is never easy to have your perception of ability shattered the way the first HL Math text does, and no one prepares you for the inevitable questioning of one's intelligence. As any HL Math student will tell you, we have all asked the same, age-old question during the 2-year course. *Am I good enough for this?*

The key to success in HL Mathematics, however, is to take the test with its big red 54% and put it on your wall. The key is to look at that score and to associate with it a sense of determination. *I will always be more prepared than I was this time.* At first it is difficult, to fall from being a model math student to scoring so low, but as with most weaknesses, the first step to improving is realizing that one has a weakness.

Even then, it is easy to say you will prepare, work and improve, but not follow through. The more difficult task is to decide on a course of action, and stick to it rigorously, rather than fooling yourself into a false sense of confidence. Remember, confidence alone scores about zero marks. Practice, on the other hand, is far more valuable.

04h30 A.M. The sun hasn't come out and the birds aren't singing because they, like the rest of your family, are asleep. Why aren't you? Sometimes it is very easy to not set aside enough time for practicing mathematics. Sometimes you are just too tired after basketball practice, or band, or just doing all of your homework, to sit down and tackle a problem that continually eludes you. Convenience and cognitive clarity are what make the morning perfect for mathematics. A solid 90 minutes of work every morning from 0430-0600 were the only reason I was able to surpass my 54% and attain an excellent grade in the final exams. By using a time of day when you are normally free and your mind is clear, you are able to reap the maximum reward in terms of improvement in your mathematics. It will be tough to wake up initially, but when your scores start rising, you'll appreciate every sleep-depriving minute.

General Tips

Studying tips:
- Your fundamental **understanding** is very important. Focus on learning the techniques you may need. There may be some techniques/tricks/solutions that your textbooks don't cover, and you can learn these from doing past papers.
- Complex numbers and planes usually have big questions in Section B, and with a bit of practice, they're pretty straightforward. I would recommend learning those topics well. Calculus comes up a fair bit, as does stats, but from my experience, complex numbers and planes are the most common.
- I generally feel that the textbooks for HL Maths do have some limitations - the questions you get in them and in real exams are quite different. I say this because I've learnt so many more 'tricks' to solving questions from exams than I have from textbooks. As such, I felt doing homework from my textbook

170

sometimes wasn't very productive. See if you can persuade your teacher to make your homework past paper questions instead of textbook questions. See next point.

- When you first start revising, I suggest using the question bank. Pick the topics you are **least** comfortable with and focus on them. When you're comfortable with them, you can start doing past papers. It's fine to repeat past papers to really drill them into yourself, some questions are kind of recycled with different numbers (e.g. complex numbers with binomial expansion). You'll get to the point where some questions are so easy that you should just skip them and do the questions that don't look easily solvable.

- As always, make sure you're focused when you're studying. Remove any sources of distractions like your phone, etc.

- There are some tiny bits of rote learning you need to do, such as the equations for sums and products of polynomials. Make sure you learn the equations for them - if you get a question on it in the exam it'll most likely be very straightforward, but if you don't know them then you've just lost some easy marks.

- Work hard on your Exploration (IA) and try and get the highest mark you can for it. I got 17/20 on my IA which really helped me. It's good to walk into the exam knowing you have a good buffer.

- Work with friends. You may not always have the best, or even right approach to a question - and they might. Sometimes it's the other way around. However, if you can explain a question to a friend and if they can understand it, then it means you know the topic well.

- It is very difficult to cram maths and I would strongly advise against it. Start revising early so you're in good shape for the exam.

<u>Exam tips:</u>

- In the real exam, you get 5 minutes reading time. Use this time to flick through every question, and make a (mental) note of the questions that are the easiest. When you can start writing, do those questions first, then do the rest of the paper. Since you have seen all the questions briefly before you begin, your brain will think in the background about these questions. You may have a sudden 'Got it!' moment for some of the harder questions even if you aren't on those questions. Two more reasons for doing this - you build up momentum and confidence and if you don't finish on time, you've maximised the amount of marks you can get.

- Don't freak out when you see a question you don't know how to do immediately, but skip it and save it for later. There was a question in my maths exam involving a goat which really tripped me up. I only did part of the question but looking back at it, it wasn't that hard a question, and I knew all the maths I needed to solve it.

- If you're stuck, flick through the formula booklet. Formula booklet is your best friend. You may see a formula that suddenly makes you understand what the question wants.

- Draw a diagram to help you picture the scenario - this is particularly helpful when doing trig, complex numbers, stats or vectors and planes.

- If you're ever substituting, which is very often, put brackets around what you have substituted in. This helps you avoid BIDMAS errors. Negative signs are a pain and doing this makes things a bit clearer. It's a good habit to get into.

- Learn how to use your GDC well. In the calculator paper there are some very easy questions if you know how to use your GDC. They're very quick and easy to do.

- Most importantly, **RTFQ. Read the full question.**

33.Mastering the Math IA [part I]

This chapter will help you achieve a minimum level 5 grade (such as 12/20) with relative ease. To score that magical mark of a 18/20 you will need to put in some effort. This guide will ensure that when you aim for those top grades that you do not lose any marks for not having conformed to both the implicit and explicit demands of the IB, no matter how small or large.

Another point to note is that this guide is written specifically for HL mathematics students but all of the points discussed also apply to Mathematics SL (I've checked and asked top scoring Mathematics SL students for their advice). I'll however add an extra section at the end highlighting the major differences between the Math HL IA and the Math SL IA.

Criteria A, Communication:

Achievement level	Descriptor
0	The exploration does not reach the standard described by the descriptors below.
1	The exploration has some coherence.
2	The exploration has some coherence and shows some organization.
3	The exploration is coherent and well organized.
4	The exploration is coherent, well organized, concise and complete.

This is probably the easiest criterion to score highly in, so follow the points below:

- **Readability, the art of making your work easy and fun to read**:
  - Proof-read your work; look for spelling mistakes and ensure that you keep your language concise and effective. Keep an eye out for the flow of the text and make sure that your sentences are well structured and easy to follow. I suggest that after you have proof-read yourself, ask one of you friends

to go over your work (tell them to keep an eye out for all the above).

- o Use interesting language, but don't saturate your work with irrelevant and fancy terms that do not belong there.
- o Keep things concise; don't go rambling on about random mildly related stuff. Try to avoid repeating yourself, and keep your work under 12 pages.

- **Structure, to stop examiners from getting confused:**
    - o Have a table of contents, and learn how to use it in MS Word. This means you should get acquainted with Text Styles (e.g. heading 1, heading 2, title and so on…).
    - o Use the in-built equation builder when you use maths in your IA. I also suggest changing the colour of the font (black for standard text, blue for math equations).
    - o Intro, Content, Conclusion. The intro should contain the reasons behind why you are interested in the topic, your IA's aim, how your topic is important on the global scale and a general overview of it. The content should have all the meaty maths (obviously) and the conclusion should have a wrap up of the exploration as well as reflection.
- **Citations, to stop you from failing the IB:**
    - o Be sure to use MLA citations (or other recognized methods by the IB) on any text or work you extract from textbooks, the Internet or whatever medium you employ.
- **Explain: show the examiner you know what you are talking about:**

- o Nearly each mathematical step in the exploration should have at least one line of text explaining what you have done.
- o If you use any non-IB mathematical knowledge be sure to spend some time explaining it.
- o If you use any non-mathematical knowledge (e.g. physics or economics), make certain that you explain it thoroughly so that your examiner is on the same level of understanding.

Criteria B, Mathematical Presentation

Achievement level	Descriptor
0	The exploration does not reach the standard described by the descriptors below.
1	There is some appropriate mathematical presentation.
2	The mathematical presentation is mostly appropriate.
3	The mathematical presentation is appropriate throughout.

This is where people lose stupid marks, so pay attention.

- **Make your work pretty, to stop any possible confusion:**
  - o Be sure that you use Insert Equations option (learn to use it, it's pretty simple and straightforward).
  - o Use different text for the math equations; make the text Italic and change its colour.
- **Use Appropriate Notation:**
  - o Never use notation that some calculations and computer software employ to denote 10^x by Ex; instead write it as a power of 10. So 3E3.5 would become $3 \times 10^{3.5}$
  - o Just use correct mathematical notation and when in doubt ask around.
- **Label Everything:**

- o If you are using generic equations make sure you label them with a line of text. This label should contain the name of the equation (as well as anything else you find appropriate).
- o Be sure to label tables and graphs using the citation tool provided by MS word. The citation should demark each element cited by a unique tag and a short explanation (e.g. table1: data from plant growth experiment // figure 1: graph of time vs acceleration).
- o When you use a table or graph make sure that they are correctly constructed. (Think of your Science IAs)
  - Tables: All rows are correctly titled, units of measurement are given (if appropriate), and all data is kept to appropriate significant figures
  - Graphs: Label all the axis, title and give units of measurement.
- **Term Definition: define fancy and complex words:**
  - o Define mathematical terms that are not common knowledge and other complex scientific or mathematical terminology. When in doubt, just define.

Criteria C, Personal engagement

Achievement level	Descriptor
0	The exploration does not reach the standard described by the descriptors below.
1	There is evidence of limited or superficial personal engagement.
2	There is evidence of some personal engagement.
3	There is evidence of significant personal engagement.
4	There is abundant evidence of outstanding personal engagement.

This criterion is a little more devious than it seems at first glance. 4 marks for showing that you care: really? Well this is how it works: if you show that you care and that you have put a lot of effort into your work you can score a maximum of 2-3/4. To get that extra four, your work needs to be solidly on point; not only do you need to show that you are "personally engaged", but your exploration also has to be of top quality. I would look at this criteria as the "holistic criteria", one in which the examiners can mark on a whim.

- **Interest is Gold (Show it or Pretend):**
    - In the introduction spend a few lines explaining why your exploration is important to you on a personal level and why you chose it. If you don't have any good answers, just lie and try to link the problem you are analysing with a personal anecdote.
- **Pick an Interesting topic: it makes it more interesting for you and your examiner:**
    - Don't select a standard textbook problem (for example solving a Rubik's cube or generic problems like that). Try to explore new problems and make your topic more interesting. By showing that you have taken the time to investigate something unusual you are demonstrating to your examiners that you are engaged and willing to learn, scoring you well in this criteria. I'll come to selecting the thesis later on in this guide.
    - Extend you mathematics beyond the obvious. Try to spend some time to see how the mathematics you are intending to use can be implemented. Show the generic solution (by generic, I mean "most obvious" or "standard" solution) and spend time attempting a non-generic solution. Even if you can't directly do the maths, talk about alternative methods for solving your

177

problem and describe in detail how it would be done. This shows the examiner you are thinking above and beyond the call of duty. Trust me, do it.

Criteria D, Reflection

Achievement level	Descriptor
0	The exploration does not reach the standard described by the descriptors below.
1	There is evidence of limited or superficial reflection.
2	There is evidence of meaningful reflection.
3	There is substantial evidence of critical reflection.

You don't get more IB than reflections and evaluations. Be sure to be efficient with your words and constantly talk about any assumptions you make.

- **Improving the exploration:**
  - o Discuss what limitation you came across when doing your IA. These limitations could be, but are not limited to the following: Time constraints (what would you have done with more time, what would you have expanded on?), lack of technology or software (how would better tools have helped you?), limitations in math skills (if you were a super mathematician what would you have done differently).
  - o Mention what other types of math you could have used to improve your explorations quality. Please note that throughout the reflection process you will have to explain things in plain English, but you should also describe and show small snippets of mathematics, here and there.
- Local and global application:
  - o You should expand on why you chose this topic and how it has implications to you personally, but most importantly, towards

humanity in general. This section should be a detailed continuation of the rationale you started in the introduction (explaining why your exploration is important on a global scale), however this time include your findings from the exploration into the analysis.

o Explain in detail how the maths and the problems you have explored are applied in the real world. Use these terms to guide you: implications, applications, limitations, compare and contrast. Think of the past, present and future, and how your exploration has changed over time (both in evolving and relevance).

- Wrap it all up
    o Create a swift conclusion that wraps up all your findings, connecting them with the reflection. The reflection will serve as a conclusion in itself; that's why no more than a paragraph is required to wrap things up.

Criteria E, Use of mathematics

Achievement level	Descriptor
0	The exploration does not reach the standard described by the descriptors below.
1	Some relevant mathematics is used. Limited understanding is demonstrated.
2	Some relevant mathematics is used. The mathematics explored is partially correct. Some knowledge and understanding are demonstrated.
3	Relevant mathematics commensurate with the level of the course is used. The mathematics explored is correct. Good knowledge and understanding are demonstrated.
4	Relevant mathematics commensurate with the level of the course is used. The mathematics explored is correct and reflects the sophistication expected. Good knowledge and understanding are demonstrated.
5	Relevant mathematics commensurate with the level of the course is used. The mathematics explored is correct and reflects the sophistication and rigour expected. Thorough knowledge and understanding are demonstrated.
6	Relevant mathematics commensurate with the level of the course is used. The mathematics explored is precise and reflects the sophistication and rigour expected. Thorough knowledge and understanding are demonstrated

This is the toughest criterion to break. Up until now you could theoretically score rather well without having much mathematical knowledge, however things here begin to change.

- **Selecting the aim**:
  - Selecting the thesis/aim of the exploration is one of the toughest yet most important parts of the IA. You must do one of the following (trust me, a failure to do so will result in poor marks): either select an original problem and solve it with traditional math, or select a traditional problem and solve it with original math (or an original problem with original math).
  - I suggest you take a problem and model it in real life (Calculus usually comes in handy here). I modelled the fuel consumption of a rocket going into orbit, and I'm also certain that almost all my calculations were incorrect, yet I still got a 18/20. The fact is that it really doesn't matter if you get the right answer; how will they ever know (unless there is a well-known answer to your problem)? As long as your mathematics is correct, it's all good. I suggest you look at mainly the modelling problems. These are the best and easiest to score highly in (as long as you follow this guide).

- **Getting more than a 4/6**
  - You cannot score more than a 4/6 by applying HL textbook math (if you are an HL student). What I did in my exploration was use integration, complex and fiddly integration. Most importantly I self-taught integration (we hadn't gone over it in class yet) and made note of it in my introduction

(I explained that I had self-taught as the IA was written before my lessons in integration) to show that I was going above and beyond. I suggest that you use advanced concepts that are taught in the course and apply them in an interesting manner. Alternatively you can learn new mathematical theorems and concepts and apply those (a problem is that most people learn new maths and don't explore it in enough depth causing low marks). If you do select a new domain of mathematics, be sure to research it well enough (you should be able to go beyond copying a Wikipedia page).

- o Don't overcomplicate your exploration for no reason. Randomly shoving formulas here and there won't help you. Actually, the randomness of these formulas will cause the flow of the exploration to break, which will cause your communication mark to go down.
- Mix it up:
  - o Within one exploration you can try different mathematical approaches to solving a problem and compare them. This type of IA would score highly on reflection and if the math is good, it would also score highly in the maths criteria.
  - o To mix it up in my IA, I combined both algebraic solutions with technological ones (using cool software). This is really good if done correctly (you must include solving by hand and algebraic solutions), however you will score extremely poorly if all calculations are done using a computer and brute force techniques.

HL vs SL

So everything is exactly the same between the two explorations in terms of IB requirements and the criteria you are targeting. The major difference comes with the mathematics you employ and their relevance. Something that would score highly on a SL exploration would not necessarily on a HL exploration (but HL will usually score extremely highly for SL). It is therefore important that you use appropriate mathematics and seek appropriate depth in you exploration. The mathematics you employ should always be on the upper difficulty limit of what you are studying, or even beyond it.

34. Mastering the Math IA [Part II – Example]

(contributed article)

Let's take for example a modelling IA, one where we want to model the Formula 1 racing and calculate the optimal strategy for it. We would want to take two opposing strategies and model their behaviour, compare them and derive an optimal solution. Please note that the points below are only summaries of possible discussion themes:

Introduction:

- Why Formula 1 interests me or a personal anecdote -(you could lie)
- If better algorithms are developed for Formula 1, these are likely to have a global effect. Technology and innovations from Formula 1 are often used in commercial situations. If efficient driving strategies are found they could be applied to smart cars (especially now that driverless cars are coming out) – Note that I am trying to relate the importance of the subject to current events and a global scale.
- A general overview of Formula 1, its rules and history – No longer that four lines.

Overview:

- The variables that will be taken into consideration, and the things that will not be taken into consideration: pit-stop times, weight of fuel and its effect on speed, acceleration and deceleration at turns, speed and its effect on wheel aging (and its relation to the number of pit-stops). Things that won't be taken into consideration, overall exact path through the track (too difficult to measure), refuelling times (no longer permitted, all fuel has to be pre-loaded onto the cars). I talk about both things that are in my capacity to calculate and things that are not. I make sure to simplify the problem so that I can apply the maths to it. I can later reflect on the simplifications that were made and score points in the reflection criteria.

- Two distinct strategies will be created, strategy A and strategy B, these will then be compared and an intermediate strategy will be developed (the more optimal one). Note that we are clearly laying out the problem and saying what we are going to be doing. It is also a good idea to refer to the techniques that we will be using. We also discuss all the parameters we are going to use and how they are linked (brief overview).

  - Strategy A: The most fuel efficient speed will be chosen, its effect on fuel consumption, tire wear, pit stops will be considered. All this data will be aggregated into a time for an arbitrary lap. The strategies effectiveness will be considered for different types of tracks.

  - Strategy B: The fastest speed will be chosen, its effect on fuel consumption (initial amount of fuel), tire wear, pit stops will be considered. All this data will be aggregated into a time for an arbitrary lap. Track length will also be considered. The strategies effectiveness will be considered for different types of tracks.

  - Strategy C: Integration and optimisation will be heavily used to find an optimal solution for finishing with the optimal time.

Mathematics:

- Option A is considered. All the mathematics is applied. The mathematics I would apply in general

184

would be calculus, particularly the domains of integration, derivation and related rates. I would have a look into Calculus options text books, and attempt to use the maths from there. I would also search the internet for interesting applications of related rates and calculus.

- Option B is considered.
- Evaluation compares A and B. Further maths are explored to combine the two strategies and develop and optional solution C. Breaking the problem down into smaller chunks and applying simple IB calculus to it can actually yield an interesting results, especially when everything is brought together into a general model. This can score you highly in the mathematics criteria as you are showing deep understanding of the problem and are applying solutions in an original manner.

Evaluation:

- Discussing potential flaws in my findings, such as the fact that the values used for tire wear, fuel consumption curves might have been wrong. You have to be critical with your own investigation, take it apart. It is completely possible you say that your results were invalid, it shows that you understand the complexity of the problem (you will get many marks for your critical thinking and actually conducting "research/exploration").
- Points that could be added to my exploration on Formula 1 racing strategy are path calculations throughout the track. If my mathematical abilities were better I could create an algorithm for path calculation. This is an art however and entire teams spend years optimising path strategies. You should discuss possible areas of expansion, even if they are not feasible. Make sure that you at least have two

feasible points and one non feasible point of expansion.

- I would talk about the global application of my exploration. The efficiency algorithms could define how cars must move for optimal efficiency. This has possible application in smart cars (cars with cruise control and lane detection) or driverless ones. The algorithms for efficiency could also be applied to other intelligent systems that move, such as: robots, UAVs and so on… Link your exploration to one closely related domain and a few distant ones.

- Calculus used in this modelling exploration is used in many domains of movement modelling such as aeronautics, space travel and even ballistics. Discuss the general application of the maths you used in the real world. It should be short, no longer than three sentences.

Cite your Sources

- Cite sources – Use MLA.

How you approach the IA

Understand:

Read the criteria and all the information that has been provided by this guide. I suggest you read it twice so to be sure that you know exactly what is expected of you. You should also consistently refer back to the guide and the criteria to refresh your memory. Try to get your hands on as many past IA examples as possible – online, or ask your school for help.

Brainstorm:

Think of your interests and hobbies, draw them out on a mind map and start connecting things together. Write down any ideas or domains of exploration that might be interesting. Once you have a few interesting problems written down, think of the mathematics that could be applied to them. Have a quick look through your text book and the Internet to gauge the difficulty of the maths. If the maths looks too difficult and undoable, don't do the problem and select a different one.

An alternative method for selecting a thesis is to first select the mathematics you wish to use, e.g. a particular domain or theory. Once that's done, you should research how this theory can be applied or think of some real life problems that could be solved using this piece of mathematics. Try to think out of the box and come up with original ideas. You will have to sit down and spend some serious time thinking of a thesis (it's one of the hardest parts).

Research:

Spend a long time becoming an expert with both your problem and the maths you will be applying to it. I suggest you use the Internet to search around for the information on your particular problem. YouTube, online archive, Wikipedia (you know what to do). For the maths however I suggest you get information from the following sources: teacher, core course book, option books, YouTube, MOOCs, and other websites. It might take you some time to get familiarised with a new domain or mathematical theory, but be sure to understand what you are studying.

Maths:

Before you write the actual essay you must be sure to get the maths sorted out. Spend a few days working on the mathematics. I suggest asking other maths teachers and even fellow students to review your work. To get a 7 or high 6 you need to spend a few days working on the maths, however if you are aiming for a 5, you can get through all the required maths in a few hours.

If you can't solve the maths however, it's time to go back a few steps and select a different thesis.

Write it all up:

Before you start writing anything be sure to reread the criteria and the guide. Now apply all the information you have learned over the last few pages and right up your exploration. This is the most tedious, but also the easiest part of the process.

Conclusion

You should also be able to get at least a 5 without much effort if you follow the tips above. Not much relies on your mathematical knowledge. Just be sure to check all the boxes and you will be ready. As a matter of fact, the guide was structured as a check list, so be sure to go through the guide and physically check off each bullet point!

I suggest that you keep an eye out for modelling problems; these can score really well as the mathematics used is not too complex yet can create depth in your Exploration.

All in all the Mathematics Internal Assessment is rather simple, follow the points discussed above and you will smash it. I suggest picking something that interests you, so that you may invest time into your work without getting bored.

35.Hacking Your GDC

The purpose of this chapter is to drill into your head that your graphing display calculator can be a tool of great importance – if you use it correctly and to its full potential. Unfortunately, because there are so many different types of graphing calculators, it will be difficult to go in depth about the secret functions of each one, but I will try to provide a resource where available.

The single best resource that can be found for all basic calculator uses in the IB (Casio fx-9860G, Texas Instruments TI-84 models, Texas Instruents TI-nspire models) is at the Haese Mathematics website. Google 'Haese Mathematics IB calculator instructions' to find a 30 page pdf document that deals extensively with almost everything you need to know about your calculator.

There is also another pdf document written by Andy Kemp that deals with the TI-nspire calculator model specifically. You can find it by googling 'IB Mathematics Exam Preparation for Calculator Papers'. The OSC also sell a book that deals with using the TI-Series in IB Mathematics, but you need to purchase this and it costs 16GBP (bit steep in my honest opinion).

There are also two excellent YouTube videos that are both 40+ mins but are essential viewing if you want to understand how to get the most out of your calculator. The first is by the HKEXCEL Education Centre and is called 'How to ace your GDC calculator for IB Math', and the other is by mathsl1 channel and is called 'IB Math SL GDC Techniques for Paper 2'. I firmly believe that every IB student should spend time watching these videos as they teach you almost all of the quintessential techniques.

Basic Calculator Tips

1. Graphs displayed on a GDC may be misleading – so make sure that what you see makes sense.

2. Be sure your GDC has new batteries before your final exams.

3. As you are not allowed a GDC on Math Paper 1, the questions on this exam will focus on analytic / algebraic 'thinking' solutions. You need to practice these and simple arithmetic and algebraic computations as you won't be able to rely on a GDC.

4. On Paper 2, if you solve an equation by means of a graph on your GDC you must provide a clearly labelled sketch of the graph in your work – and indicate exactly what equation you solved on your GDC.

5. Even though a GDC is 'required' for Paper 2, do not assume that you will need to use your GDC on every question for Paper 2.

6. Do not use any calculator notation in your written solutions.

7. If you use your GDC to obtain an answer for a question on Paper 2, be sure that you clearly write down the appropriate mathematical 'set-up' for the computation you will perform on your GDC.

8. There will inevitably be some questions on Paper 2 where it will be more efficient to find the answer by using your GDC as oppose to an analytic method. Do not lose valuable time by choosing to answer a question using a tedious analytic method when you could get the answer quickly with your GDC.

GDC in IA / EE

If you have the opportunity to use your GDC graphs in your mathematics exploration or mathematics EE (if you are doing one), I would highly suggest this. It looks very impressive, and it shows examiners that you are using the tools at your disposal. Your calculator should have come with a USB link to your computer and software to extract the graphs / calculations – explore these avenues.

Formula Booklet

I want to take a section of this chapter to also stress the importance of knowing your math formula booklet inside out. During exams it is absolutely essential that students know where to quickly find every formula. Saving time by knowing where to find necessary equations in the data booklet and how to perform shortcuts on the calculator allows for extra time to solve the questions themselves and double-check over work. You don't want to be spending extra time looking for that one equation only to realize that it's not in the formula booklet, or not know how to perform an essential function on your calculator.

Being familiar with the formula booklet is even more important considering that several useful equations are missing from the formula booklet, and several difficult-to-remember equations are included. Students should therefore know which equations they will need to memorize and which are easily accessible. For example, in the HL and Further HL formula booklet there is the formula for the angle between two vectors, but not between two planes or a vector and a plane.

Smartib Formula Booklet

We are developing in-app formula IB booklets for the smartib app, so hopefully this will be out very soon – keep your eyes open for this update.

36. Acing Visual Art

(contributed article)

I got a level 7 HL Visual Art this year and I have some important advice. I was looking for it when I was working, all over the internet and all I got was a regurgitated syllabus (or maybe repetition of what teachers has said...). So here it goes:

1. Pretend you are not doing the IB or any equivalent of school work (if you did GCSEs, forget anything connected to the format or requirements.) The IB as you should know has no prescribed themes; teachers usually try to make you set yourself limits. Resist. It's the one good thing about the actual visual arts course.

2. Culture is such a big word in the IB, but it doesn't have to mean worship and political correctness. If you really are a 'world student' and a thinker and all those other IB don't be afraid to criticise another culture as well as your own. You will not be penalised for having a voice as long as you know what you are talking about. Also don't focus on it too much I've seen a lot of people obsessing about the culture aspect and it is so false and forced. If you don't feel it, aren't really that interested in it, then do not do it. My work was all universal - apart from literally 4 sketchbook pages on voodoo.

3. Other Artists: mention many but I beg you, again, do not force or obsess. Some projects come from you! Why should everything be an inspiration by Picasso or Rothko etc. It shouldn't work like this - you are in the driving seat. When I mentioned artists it was usually because of how they worked - method or how they thought that was inspiring; I tried to explain this well, and also explain why my work looks nothing like theirs and is absolutely unconnected in theme. If

you know your art history and theory well by reading in spare time, gallery's etc. this can work for you.

4. Studio Work is what makes you get a level 7 or so I believe, this is where the goods and time must lie whatever Option you take. It's what makes a real artist- I know a girl who got a level 5 - I was shocked! Her sketchbooks were the most beautiful, original and amazing things I have ever seen (god I was jealous), have never seen better even on university level but the final pieces were average. I would recommend academic sculpting-its very time consuming but I recommend you do this in year 13 if you are confident painter/drawer, it's also something fun and gives you a break from the whole paper format.

5. SKETCH BOOKS. The most difficult part for me as I hated having to be in a prescribed format (I generally hate rules I didn't make up) and I am a horrible perfectionist. I will be honest with you; I ripped many pages, stuck many together and repainted over others. I don't believe mistakes are a very good thing. For me it is weakness, the learning experience is when you learn to do the page better and when your next RWB has less of those mistakes (yes my teacher was angry - but doesn't everyone hate ugly pages? they are not ok). But do not make this mistake which I did, get obsessed about one pages and do it 10 times over chances are after the second time it will not improve much and is just a waste of time.

6. If you too hate sketchbooks I have a recommendation, carry around a moleskin/ small notebook where you really can have a diary/ note pad/ mini sketchbook with no rules. Scan the pages from it that are nice and pretty or have interesting ideas, insights into your work and stick them into your RWB. This went down a hit with every one, moderater,examiner. + present the originals at interview, exhibit and send to moderater (if your school requires it like mine did) it counts as extra work and is very personal and shows your serious.

7. The interview is not difficult - if you know about your subject, mine ended up being less about all my work than about my attitude towards art. You can steer the conversation in a direction you would like by talking about things that will make the examiner interested to question you further.

IWB Advice

One of the biggest problems I have seen students encounter in their IB1 and IB2 with IB Visual Arts is their **workbooks**. Below I wish to give advice on how to complete amazing workbooks pages that relate to your studio works. All of the information below is from my personal experience and from watching other IB students in visual arts who have received 6s and 7s for their final IB grade. Besides giving simple advice, I have reviewed the syllabus, and I will try to demonstrate how the advice and tips given relate to what is said in the syllabus about requirements, objectives, outcomes, etc.

Investigation Criteria for Full Markings (OFFICIAL IB SYLLABUS EXCERPT)
- Analyses and compares perceptively art from different cultures and times, and considers it thoughtfully for its function and significance.
- Demonstrates the development of an appropriate range of effective skills, techniques and processes when making and analyzing images and artifacts.
- Demonstrates coherent, focused and individual investigative strategies into visual qualities, ideas and their contexts, an appropriate range of different approaches towards their study, and some fresh connections between them.
- Demonstrates considerable depth and breadth through the successful development and synthesis of ideas and thoroughly explained connections between the work and that of others.

- Demonstrates effective and accurate use of the specialist vocabulary of visual arts.
- Uses an appropriate range of sources and acknowledges them properly.
- Presents the work effectively and creatively and demonstrates effective critical observation, reflection and discrimination.
- Presents a close relationship between investigation and studio.
-

Workbook, not a Sketchbook

The IBO refers to the sketchbooks used for your IB Visual Arts, both Standard Level and Higher Level as a **Workbook** or**Investigation Workbook.** There is a subtle reason for this change in name. Typically, a sketchbook is filled with random sketches, drawings, paintings, etc.; meanwhile, the IB Visual Arts Workbook also **focuses on a writing aspect.**

Your workbook pages, no matter how creative, will not be solid if the pages do not also contain writing with explanations for your drawings, brainstorming, etc. Therefore, for **the amount of drawing/sketching you put into your workbook, you should have a solid amount of writing/explanation on the same page** to go with it.

In your recorded Interview, it is a good idea to present your IWB and flip through your pages as you explain your work. The camera can zoom to film close up of specific things you are talking about. Some people like to fill up a page with drawings from their brainstorming, and then write another page about it. But that is not the most effective way. When the interviewer looks at one of your workbooks pages he/she wants to be able to read about how your sketch(es) relate to your plan of working, inspiration, ideas, artists you are looking into, etc. It must be a TRUE INVESTIGATION. Besides your brainstorming, experimentation, sketches and drawings, Interviewers want to see that you have investigated the techniques you are using or artists you are imitating. Make sure that for every studio work you create, you have a solid amount of INVESTIGATORY EXPLANATIONS in your workbooks.

The purpose of the investigation workbooks is to encourage personal investigation into visual arts, which must be closely related to the studio work undertaken. The relative importance of the investigation workbooks depends on whether the student has chosen option A or option B.

The investigation workbooks should incorporate contextual, visual and critical investigation. They should function as working documents and support the student's independent, informed investigation and studio practice. Investigation workbooks provide an opportunity for reflection and discovery and they play a key role in allowing ideas to take shape and grow. They should contain visual and written material that addresses contextual, visual and critical aspects of the investigation. They should also reflect the student's interests and include wide-ranging first-hand investigations into issues and ideas related to visual arts. There should be a balance in the investigation between analytical and open-ended discussion, illustrating the student's creative thinking.

Quantity AND Quality

Many students think that they can get by with minimal sketchbooks pages, as long as the quality is sufficient. If you want to score 4, that will work.

If you want to score over 4, you must do MORE THAN THE MINIMUM. When you present your studio works and investigation workbooks in your video, the examiner will want to be able to see more pages than just the ones you turned in as your main pages. They want to see investigations, experimentation and drawings that you looked into, **even if you did not use** those newly learned skills or factual information in your final studio works. This demonstrates to the interviewer that you are not just meeting the criteria from the IB Visual Arts Syllabus, but you are going the extra mile. For a certain studio work, you may turn in 3 pages from your investigation workbooks about it, but the interviewer will want to see more. Even if you have one extra page, two, five or fifteen, **displaying extra knowledge that you did not turn in is vital.** After all, you are turning in your main pages, not all of the pages related to one of you main studio works.

You should be completing about 2 workbook pages a week. So let's do the math: if there are approximately 36 weeks in one school year, and the IB Visual Arts Program is two years, you have 72 weeks of school. 72 x 2= 144. Therefore, you should have a minimum of about **144 workbook pages** when it is time for your art interview! This is a lot, but it is doable if you stay on track!

AREAS TO CONSIDER

- There are five common functions of art: **Personal, Social, Spiritual, Educational and Political**. Your studio works should strive to encompass more than one of these areas, but you are not required to do all of the areas.
- **Personal Relevance:** to express personal feelings. Perhaps the artist wanted to remind viewers of personal family tragedy, or perhaps he just wanted to tell them to appreciate what they had, and to live each day as if it were their last.
- **Social/Cultural Relevance:** to reinforce and enhance the shared sense of identity of those in family, community, or civilization, for example, festive occasions, parades, dances, uniforms, important holidays or events.
- **Spiritual Relevance:** to express spiritual beliefs about the destiny of life controlled by the force of a higher power.
- **Educational Relevance:** symbols and signs to illustrate knowledge not given in words

- **Political Relevance:** to reinforce and enhance a sense of identity and ideological connection to specific political views, parties and/or people.

This is how I generally set the workbook pages for my studio works. It is an easy outline to follow, and it keeps me organized. It also demonstrates to the interviewer that I have a consistent train-of-thought when I pursue a new studio work. This is from my personal experience. No such outline is recommended or required by the IBO. Also, if you have found your own outline that works for you, this one is not necessarily better. The final outline is up to you. Your teacher is asking for about TWO solid, good, creative workbook pages a week with a project every FOUR weeks, therefore I designed my own outline to give me 6+ sketchbooks pages. The remaining pages I usually fill with other artists, random experimentation, etc. (depending on what I feel I am lacking in my workbook)

Outline and Explanation:
1. **Introduction Pages**- Introduce the ISSUE/IDEA/THEME that you plan on exploring, investigating, brainstorming and creating. Explain why you are interested in that idea. This may include a definition of the issue, background information, a few minor sketches of how you visualize the issue/theme/idea.
2. **Inspirations (Artist) Pages**- Introduce the artists that are inspiring you. Not all studio works will have the artists page because you may use one artist inspiration for more than one studio piece or you may not have had a specific artist that inspired you for that specific studio work. You may also find yourself inspired by a historical event, a field trip, a collection of photos, a current event..... Briefly write factual information about the artist (this writing should be in the minority). Sketch out some of his/her works or glue in pictures if it is too difficult to imitate their works. Explain how their art

198

has inspired you and how you plan to use that inspiration in your studio work(s) (this writing should be in the majority). You do not have to imitate the artists technique to use them as an inspirational figure. You could have been inspired by the themes they target, sizes of art they create, their morals and/or beliefs, etc. Make sure to mention what aspect about the artist inspired you!

3. **Brainstorming Pages**- brainstorm your ideas. The brainstorming pages should turn into 3-4 pages depending on how simple or complex the studio work idea is. Write about technique ideas, media ideas, area(s) you wish to target, etc. Give about 3+ different compositional ideas you have in your mind about creating the studio work and how you envision the final piece. Another good idea is to draw out the materials you are thinking about using, instead of gluing in pictures of them. At the end of the brainstorming page write about which ideas you are looking into pursuing the most. Use colors, underlining, etc. to indicate minor ideas versus major ideas.

4. **Experimentation Pages**- Experiment in your workbook with the mediums/colour schemes/techniques/ your wish to incorporate into your studio piece. The experimentation page typically turns into two or three pages. Make the experimentation the main part of the page and leave a corner or strip of the page to explain yourself (do you like the media/technique, how did the experimentation go, define what you mean by bad or good experimentation, do you plan on using this technique for your studio work or have you decided on another, why or why not have you chosen this media/technique, etc.). Write you explanation in paragraph or bullet-point format. Do not write out questions you are answering and then the answers.

5. **Process Pages**- have someone take pictures randomly throughout your creation of the studio

work so you can glue them onto your process page. Reflect on the pictures (what are you doing in the photographs, are you having trouble, are you doing well, are you satisfied with your progress, etc.)

6. **Reflection Page**- Once your studio piece is complete is it good to have a reflection page about your work. Take a picture of your final work and glue it in, then write your thoughts. Speak about the good things and the bad things, difficulties, your likes and dislikes, how you have enhanced your skill in a certain media or technique, if you are satisfied with your work and why or why not, what would you do differently if you had to do the studio piece again, etc.

7.

When you are writing in your IWB, don't forget that IB is an ACADEMIC course and that your written notes should reflect that. Describe your feelings, thoughts, successes and failures, comment upon your own progress and your ideas but DON'T use slang or informal English. Remember that this is your IWB – it's not being written for friends – an IB examiner will be reading it.

THE LANGUAGE OF ART

People throughout the world speak many different languages. To learn a new language, you need to learn new words and a new set of rules for putting those words together. The language of visual arts has its own system. They are arranged according to basic principles. As you learn these basic elements and principles, you will learn the language of art. It will increase your ability to understand, appreciate, and enjoy art, and to express yourself clearly when discussing or producing artwork. In your investigation workbooks, you should be demonstrating an increase in knowledge about the language of art. This is done through investigation pages and experimentation pages. You investigations and experimentation do not always have to be related directly to the studio piece you are working with. They could simply be for further knowledge and possible ideas for future works.

Elements of Art:
- line
- color
- form
- space
- value
- shape
- texture

Principles of Design:
- pattern
- balance
- proportion
- variety
- emphasis
- rhythm
- movement
- unity

Properties in Art
- **Subject**- is the image viewers can easily identify in a work of art. The subject may be one person or many people; it may be an event, an object, a symbol, etc. In these types of works, the elements of art themselves become the subject matter.
- **Composition**- the way the *principles* of art are used to organize the *elements* of art
- **Content**- the message the work communicates. The message may be an idea or a theme, such as family togetherness, or emotions like love, loneliness, happiness, pride, etc.

Your investigation workbook should demonstrate, **over time**, a high quality of understanding of the language of art, with respect to the elements or art, principles of design and the basic properties/features of an artwork. Do not expect to have amazing vocabulary and understanding right at the beginning of your time in IB Visual Arts. These are skills you will develop over time. The interviewers **want to see a development in your skills**. So how do you go about demonstrating an increase in knowledge about the Language of Art?

Tips for Developing your Knowledge about the Language of Art:

Investigation Pages- when investigating an artist, look up new vocabulary (artistic words related to the form of art you are looking at). Create a investigation workbook page about it and write about it. One thing I always added in was a corner in the page called: "New Glossary Terms", where I would list new words I learned and their brief definition. Feel free to create investigation pages throughout your workbook that are unrelated to your current studio piece you are working on.

Experimentation Pages- when experimenting with a new technique or medium, make sure to check up the actual terminology for them. Like the investigation pages, write up the new vocabulary and their brief definitions. This will demonstrate to the interviewer that you recognized new vocabulary linked to a specific medium and technique and that you have taken note of it. Make sure to use that new vocabulary throughout the rest of your investigation workbook if you use that technique or medium. The interviewer likes to see how you have learned new, important words, and strive to use them when explaining your own art.

GUIDED QUESTIONS FOR ANALYZING OTHER ARTISTS' ARTWORKS
First Reaction- write down your first response to the artwork
- Did you like it?
- How does it make you feel?
- Does it remind you of anything you have seen before?

Description- list what you can see in this artwork
- Figures, colors, shapes, objects, background, etc.
- Imagine you are describing it to a blind person. Do this in as much detail as possible

Formal Analysis- write down your observations in more detail, looking at these specific aspects of the artwork:
- **Colors:**
  - Which type of palette has the artist used: is it bright or dull, strong or weak?
  - Are the colors mostly complementary, primary, secondary or tertiary?
  - Which colors are used most, and which are used least in this artwork?
  - Are the colors used different ways in different parts of the artwork?
  - Have the colors been applied flat (straight from the tube), or have different colors been mixed?
- **Tones:**
  - Is there a use of light/shadow in this artwork?
  - Where is the light coming from? where are the shadows?
  - Are the forms in the artwork realistically modeled (does it look 3D)?
  - Is there a wide range of tonal contrast (very light highlights and very dark shadows) or is the tonal range quite narrow (mostly similar tones)?
- **Use of Media:**
  - What medium has been used?
  - How has the artist used the medium (applied thick or thin? How can you tell?)
  - Can you see brushstrokes, markmaking or texture? Describe the shape and direction of the brushstrokes/marks. What size of brush.pencil was used?
  - Was is painted, drawn, sculpted quickly, or slowly? What makes you think this?

- **Composition:**
  - What type of shapes are used in this artwork? (rounded, geometric, curved, etc.)
  - Is there a mixture of different types of shapes or are all of the shapes similar?
  - Are some parts of the composition full of shapes and some empty or are the shapes spread evenly across the artwork?
  - Are some shapes repeated or echoed in other parts of the artwork?
  - Does the whole composition look full of energy and movement, or does it look still and peaceful?
  - How did the artist create this movement or stillness?
  - What is the center of interest in the composition?
  - How does the artist draw your attention to it?
- **Mood/Emotion:**
  - What do you think the artist wanted you to feel when you look at this artwork?
  - What has he/she used to create a mood? (think about the colors, shapes, tones, etc.)
  - How has he/she succeeded in creating this mood?

Interpretation- your personal thoughts about the work

- What do you think the artist is trying to say in this artwork? What does it mean?
- What is the main theme or idea behind this piece?
- If you were inside this artwork, what would you be feeling / thinking?
- Does the artwork have a narrative (tell a story)? is it a religious artwork?
- Is it abstract? Is it realistic? Why?
- How would you explain this artwork to someone else?

Evaluation- based on what you have observed, give your opinion of the artwork with reasons

- Is it successful or not? Why?

GUIDED QUESTIONS FOR REFLECTION ON YOUR OWN STUDIO WORK

- How do you feel overall with the studio work?
- Define what you mean by "good" or "bad" studio work?
- What difficulties did you encounter?
- How did you overcome these difficulties?
- Does the studio work look like how you imagined it?
- What would you do differently if you could do it over again?
- What is your favorite part about your final studio piece?
-

EXTRA PAGE IDEAS

When I first enter the IB Visual Arts program, I was really confused as to what different things I can put into my workbook. At the beginning of IB1, I experimented a lot with different types of pages to see what comments I would receive from my teacher. By the end of my first semester, I compiled a list of good types of workbook pages that received good comments. I continue to utilize that list whenever I feel that I am missing something in my workbook. For all of you who are not quite sure what you can include into your own workbooks, here is the list I compiled, so it may give you some useful ideas:

- **Artist Page**- a page in your sketchbook researching a specific artist of your interest. This page usually contains a creative title (decorated artist's name, decorated piece of works name, etc.), a brief biography, reasons you chose the artist, how you plan to use the knowledge you have learned from that artist in your future works, sketches or pictures of the artist's works, etc.

- **Art Analysis Page**- this is not an "Artist Page". It focuses solely on one work from a specific artist and analyzes that work in-depth. This page is typically mostly writing with a brief sketch of the work being analyzed and a picture of the original work. See the "Questions for Analyzing Artwork" for guidance on this page.

- **Technique Experimentation Page**- this is a page filled with your experimentation with one specific technique. Commonly, this page turns into 2 or 3 pages. The reason for this is because sometimes you can experiment with the same technique using different mediums, so you may chose to experiment with 2-3 different mediums, each on its own page. Make sure to reflect on your experimentation on each page, not just the last one!

- **Medium Experimentation Page**- this is a page filled with your experimentation with one specific medium. Commonly, this page turns into 2 or 3 pages. The reason for this is because sometimes you can experiment with the same medium using different techniques, so you may chose to experiment with 2-3 different techniques, each on its own page. Make sure to reflect on your experimentation on each page, not just the last one!

- **Research Page** (other than artists)- this page is similar to the "artist page", but instead of investigation/researching one artist, you are researching one symbol, object, person, theme, etc. On this page you will, generally, draw the object, symbol, etc. being researched and write out new information you have learned about it. A good way to go about your writing on the "research page" would be to give various definitions of the object being researched- common dictionary definition, word origin and history, medical dictionary, science dictionary, famous quotes using that object, etc. Finally, form your own definition out of the researched definitions to demonstrate how you plan on using the object, symbol, etc. in your studio work(s).

- **Practicing Page**- similar to the experimentation pages, yet is related to one studio work. If you plan on using a new medium you are unfamiliar with for a studio work, it is a good idea to have 1-3 experimental pages of that medium or technique before you begin your actual studio work. If the experimentation is too large to be done in your workbook, then take pictures while experimenting (e.g. if you are experimenting with clay) and glue them on to one page in your workbook. Make sure to reflect on the experimentation!

- **TOK Link Page**- for students who are on the IB Diploma Program (not certificate program), it is important to connect your IB Visual Art experience to your TOK class. This page is simply a page with you writing about a position you take on a certain debatable/controversial topic concerning art, giving arguments, giving examples of artworks to defend your arguments, and giving a conclusion. The example artworks you use can be both in the form of picture of sketches. Of course, sketching is always more preferable, but sometimes it is difficult to imitate artworks, so feel free to use photographs. Generally, you should have a couple of these types of pages in your IB Visual Arts years. If you have 2 or 3 by the time your interview takes place, that's perfect!

Some Ideas for TOK Questions for you TOK Link Page:
- What is Art?
- Is art original?
- Is it important for artworks to be original? Why?
- Life imitates art far more than art imitates life. Explain.
- Is art a Lie or Truth? Explain.

GOOD HABITS

Work in your IWB EVERY DAY! Get into the habit, starting today! Several good IWB pages spread out over a few days work is always better than hours of late night rushed work late at night. Researching, drawing and designing your IWB pages will be an excellent creative break for you from other types of academic study – you should enjoy it! That's why you've chosen this course, right?

When you finish an IWB page, put the date including the year. This clearly shows your progress throughout the course.

When you write in your IWB use a black pen and write clearly. We have to photograph pages to send to the examiners – and they have to be able to read it. It should be an easy pleasurable read (think picture books when you were a kid... what did you like to read??!)

When drawing something from observation, automatically write down where you were and why you chose to draw that. Make notes on the weather or lighting if appropriate. Take photographs as well and attach them to the page.

When you use a book or the internet for info or pictures COPY the URL immediately. The same goes for magazines, newspapers, films, etc. You have to reference EVERYTHING.

Your IWB should reflect your personal approach and style. They are not scrapbooks or sketchbooks. Don't throw out weaker pages as this prevents your teacher and the examiner from seeing your progress. The examiners are not looking for a beautiful finished presentation, but a well worn, well used, well considered journal. Even if you don't like the results of your study, you can learn from your mistakes. And this, actually, will be more interesting to the examiner, instead of pretending that you did everything perfectly the first time around. You will need to use most of your class time for STUDIO work. Expect to do most of your IWB work outside of class.

TO GET STARTED.....

Choose an A4 sketchbook with reasonably thick white cartridge paper. This is the best size as it easily fits into your school bag and the pages aren't big enough to be overwhelmingly. Make sure you choose a spiral-bound or hard cover sketchbook (spiral is the best). Gummed sketchbooks will quickly fall apart.

Put your name and address on the inside front cover. Also a phone number – if you lose it... you will want it back!! Remember to DATE and NUMBER each page, as you work along.

LAST WORDS OF ADVICE
DON'T:

- If you mess up a page in you sketchbook do not tear it out, instead write about it, on the same page, about what you did wrong and why it failed and what you learned

- Do not feel like your art needs to based off of some deep, philosophical topic, or some huge event in society (ex. global warming, racism, rape, women's rights, etc). It is way overused and sometimes you run out of ideas, but if you have lots of ideas for something like that, go for it. For instance, I sat around for ages trying to think of a topic the interviewers would think was deep and profound, in the end, I found a simple topic where I could look into the history, society and connect it personally. I ended up taking "coffee" as a theme I use over and over again, and it allowed me to look into how it developed, social problems, addictions, etc.

- Don't use glitter in your IWB. It's not considered professional. If you want something to look shinny, find some specific paint or try to make the effect on your own.

DO:

- Always leave 1-2 pages at the beginning of your sketchbook blank in order to make a table of contents. Some students leave it at the end, don't do that. The IB interviewer should be able to open your sketchbooks first page and find what he/she wants

- Make sure to number your pages once you are done with your sketchbook
- **Put dates.** They are getting stricter in IB about having dates on each page. They'll be looking for it.
- **Reference everything**. Anything you get from books, online, etc. need to be references. Just write the name of the book, or the internet URL underneath the picture or info you are quoting or summarizing. I sometimes just put the references in a small box at the bottom of the page.

37. Excel at the Extended Essay [Part I]

Those two dreaded words. Extended Essay. The EE. Satan's Essay. Whatever you want to call it, there's no denying that amongst all the responsibilities that the IB student is expected to juggle, the compulsory EE is by far the most feared and hated. This 3,500 to 4,000 word mandatory research paper raises many eyebrows when first introduced to IB students. This is usually followed by a tiny voice in your head telling you "4,000 words on ANYTHING over two years? That's easy!" Well, you would think so, wouldn't you? Why, then, do so many IB students find themselves in the beginning of their final year without a draft, without an outline, without even a title idea?

Let's do some simple mathematics. Let's say, hypothetically, that you are given exactly a one-year deadline to finish your EE (it's around that). That's 365 days. Now let's say you are an overachiever and want to write 4,000 words (the upper limit of essay length). According to my calculations, that's 4,000 divided by 365 or around 10.95 words per day. That's it. If you write 10.95 words per day for a year, then you will have completed your extended essay. I hope most of you can manage eleven words a day.

Now, don't be fooled – I'm not suggesting you spread your EE writing exactly over a one year period – I am merely trying to show you how little 4,000 words over a year really is. As part of Economics and Management degree at Oxford, I was required to write a 3000 – 4000 word essay per week. Yup, that's right, an EE per week, and after having done it for the first few weeks, it became easier and easier up until the point where 4,000 words seemed like nothing. The IB, in an attempt to prepare you for this, generously gives you well over a year to write your "masterpiece."

What your aims are will largely depend on what you want to achieve with your EE. Considering you are actually reading this book in full, I will assume you are serious about getting that A grade that you need to get all three of your bonus points and push you closer to that magic 45. Well, then these chapters will not disappoint you. If, on the other hand, you are someone who just needs to pass the IB diploma with the minimum requirements (which involves passing the EE), you have also come to the right place.

So what is the problem then? Why do so many students struggle to write what seems to be a simple "extended" essay in such a great amount of time? Well, there are a few traps along the way, and hopefully the following guide over the next few pages will teach you how to avoid those traps and have your EE ready in no time.

What Subject?

Now, although there are no real restrictions on the nature of your essay, it must fall within a subject the IB has on offer (published by the IB in the *Vade Mecum*). Please don't be a wise-guy and try to write an essay on a subject that you do not take. Yes, it is actually allowed and I have seen it happen, at times with mediocre success, but usually with utter failure. A typical example: you are obsessed with WWI history, but your school does not teach history at all, yet you insist that your external reading you do in your own time will give you a great idea and basis for an essay. You spew out 4,000 words of something you believe is truly brilliant and hand it in to your middle school history teacher to mark. They think it's great. You then send it to the IB only to find out you completely missed the History EE guidelines and end up getting a generous grade D.

Another, more common, example is someone who is really passionate about religion and wants to do a paper in world religion. You will most likely end up being incredibly biased and perhaps say very controversial things. I'll probably regret saying this, but the EE and the IB don't deal directly with religion (unless it's the simple appreciation and acceptance of others' beliefs). Some schools have simply begun to ban their students from writing outside of their own subject areas (probably because of the lack of supervisors available). Look, you do six subjects so is it really that difficult to find something that interests you ever-so-slightly within those six?

Make sure you take a look at the detailed package of documents that the IB offers for the Extended Essay, which will include information on what you should expect in writing each essay. I'm not going to outline what the IB documents say because 1) I don't want to source things you can look up yourself and 2) you can look it up yourself! Once you have chosen your subject, you should print out the relevant guide and read it carefully. Also make sure that you have a supervisor available to oversee your EE in that subject area.

.

So, which Group should you be looking at then? Well, as my personal advice, I would tell you to stay away from any English or language essays unless you truly have a passion for literature and have been published or somehow rewarded for truly excelling in your writing. The reason is quite simple: writing an excellent literature essay is incredibly difficult because it's simply too competitive and many students who believe they are excellent writers and have been told so by numerous teachers are, in fact, quite average when compared to kids outside of their school. Do not become one of those students who say: "Hah! I'll just take one of my grade A English papers I wrote on *Doll's House* from last year, add 2000 more words and - viola! Extended Essay complete!" It does not work like that. The EE isn't really an extended essay – you can't simply elongate your normal run-of-the-mill English analysis of a literary work and expect to do well. The problem with Group 1 essays is that many will fail to reveal much personal judgement and overuse historical and biographical information. A very subtle balance is required, and this is often very difficult to maintain. EE reports show that students use secondary sources in place of personal opinions and vocabulary is often a problem, along with structure and quotations. The EE is supposed to be a piece of research, which is why I would suggest you stay away from literature because there is little research to be done.

Group 3 topics seem to make very popular EEs – and perhaps with good reason, too. There are virtually no limitations on what you can write about in Geography, Economics, Business Management, History, and so on. If you take a Group 3 topic that you are truly interested in, see if there is anything you have always pondered over but never really researched in depth. Talk to your teachers and coordinators about the success rates in these topics. For subjects like Economics and Business Management there is always great demand; however, success is varied. I remember an Economics teacher of mine told me that although it is easy to get a B or C in an Economics EE, you have to come up with pretty good material to get an A. Please, don't fall into the trap of "Oh, my dad has his own company, so what better way to do research in business/economics than to write an essay about his company!" Just because you have access to thousands of documents for a firm of a friend or a relative does not mean this will help you write an excellent essay in Economics or BM.

A common trouble area with Economics essays is that there is little personal research and not enough analysis of economic theory. Also, as you would with your Economics coursework, don't forget to define all the key economic terms (either on the spot or as an index). At all cost avoid subjective "What if.." questions because this just does not fit well with the EE's Assessment Criteria. And please, for your own good, make sure to narrow the topic down to a sort of small case study.

With regards to History essays, the problem is as you would expect: reliability of secondary sources (probably would be a good idea NOT to use too many websites). Don't forget that your bibliography for a History essay will probably be twice as long as the bibliography in any other subject – so get ready to do some serious citing. Avoid the traditional "arguments for" followed by "arguments against" approach and then a conclusion consisting of "both sides of the argument are equally valid." Yes, it would be worse to produce a one-sided argument, but avoid being too neutral as well.

What about Group 4 then, the sciences? It seems at first that the task would to be akin to a middle school science fair project or simply a longer-than-usual lab report. Don't get your hopes up. Writing an EE in a science is very demanding, as it not only requires you to have the literary ability found in any other EE, but you also must be able to master the process of conducting experiments, taking data, and providing top-of-the line analysis. My personal advice: if you are an excellent laboratory scientist with plenty of experience writing up lab reports and doing numerous research projects and you have an idea for an EE topic that is not discussed in much detail in the syllabus, then go for it. Perhaps more so than with any other group, writing an EE in Group 4 requires that you have a clear idea what you want to research. You need to know exactly what you are doing and have a pretty good idea of what will happen. Sounds a bit demanding, but there's no point in looking at "the effect of sunlight on erection length" if there's clearly no relationship between the two variables! You would be wasting your time starting to write an EE about a scientific relationship that you doubt actually exists. The flipside, however, is that you would be wasting your time doing an experiment for which the outcome is already well documented in standard textbooks. Hence, you face a dilemma.

Moreover, it is very difficult to write an essay that is distinctly a chemistry essay, not shifting over too much to biology or physics. You could end up with an essay that relates very little to your specific science subject. Again, official IB EE reports state that many science essays lack a satisfactory degree of personal input – perhaps using sophisticated lab equipment limits how much personal input one can have. You also face the risk of reaching a somewhat too general conclusion, and analysis of sources and methods used is often too weak because of the high level of sophistication.

Ah, an EE in Group 5: mathematics, computer sciences, perhaps the most overlooked EE subject area. As I have relatively little knowledge about computer sciences, I will primarily be concerned with an EE in mathematics, so any computer science students can look away now. Also, unless you are taking HL Mathematics, you can forget about writing an EE in maths as well. Now, if you are a HL Mathematics student who is not struggling too much with the material and actually enjoys mathematics, then follow my advice and do an EE in it! Trust me, it will probably be the best decision you will make in your IB experience. Yes, it seems a daunting task – how can one write 4000 words on a subject that is primarily concerned with numbers? But once you do a little research, read several past mathematics essays and convince yourself that writing an EE in maths will be no more or less challenging than any other subject, you should begin to worry less about the whole concept. You will not be expected to make a contribution to the knowledge in the mathematical world. Don't worry, they won't expect you to find the next largest prime number or solve Fermat's Theorem.

There is an unbelievable amount of resources available for anyone interested in doing an EE in mathematics. It really does shock me how few students give it a go, let alone think about doing it. In my year, it was me and only one other student that attempted the EE in mathematics (in our school). It was perhaps the most enjoyable and, at the same time, most demanding piece of work I had to do for the IB – but at the end of the day, it was something I could honestly pick up and be proud of. You don't need a Bachelor's degree in mathematics to be able to write an essay in maths. It might well be more demanding than an EE in other subject areas, but your willingness to challenge yourself will not go unrecognized by the EE examiners. Keep in mind that the minimum word limit is altered for EE in mathematics to around 2500 words (which is nothing really) but you do need a significant amount of actual maths in the text as well (which could be a problem).

What about Group 6? Well, I don't know many who have done an EE in visual arts, theatre arts or music, but if you feel you've got a mini art-critic living inside you, then give it a thought. If you plan on pursuing a university degree involved in the arts, then this may well be an opportunity to see what it would be like doing detailed research and analysis in that area. Remember that there is a great element of creativity involved, so if you're finding your Group 6 classes and assignments uninteresting, then perhaps it would be a good idea to stay away from an EE in that area. Don't think that for your art EE you can just analyze the history of graffiti or that for your music essay you can write 50 Cent's biography – it has to be of a quality expected in the IB program.

The bottom line is that you need to take a long and hard look at your HL classes and decide which subject will suit your essay needs best. I know that the emphasis on EE and subjects differs from school to school, so if you are at a school that is really science-intensive and lacking on the mathematics, then it would probably be better to follow that route. You should ensure that you write your EE at HL, not at SL – simply because you will have not learnt the subject in enough detail. If you are doing HL Mathematics, I once again strongly suggest that you at least consider writing an EE in this subject. If not, my next best bet for you would be to look at your Group 3 subjects and choose something from there. If you're more of a scientist than a social scientist, then by all means go for the Group 4; however, be warned of the obstacles and traps that you may have to overcome. Unless you are a truly naturally gifted literary critic and have extraordinary analysis skills, I would strongly advise to stay away from Groups 1 and 2. Similarly, unless you are obsessed with your Group 6 subject, I would not recommend doing an EE in the arts.

38. Excel at the Extended Essay [Part II]

Topic Choice

Once you have done the easy part of choosing under which subject your EE will fall, you must begin thinking of a topic or a range of topics that you could write about. Pick something that actually interests you and is motivating. Don't get too excited if you can find a truckload of information online about your topic of interest – that's usually a bad sign. Pick a topic that has barely any research already done on it and is unique in its nature. Remember, however, that this is a research topic and not your ordinary book review – you must have a question, which you can argue and answer.

Also remember that it needs to be very specific – you don't want a topic that is too general. Please, understand just how important your topic choice really is – it will make or break your essay. Choose something that is silly and unprofessional and you will suffer incredibly. Before you decide on a topic, talk to your friends about it, Google it, see if there's an appropriate approach that you can take. A paper on "Economic Monopolies" is far too general, but a paper on a specific type of company monopoly, analysed at a more in-depth level, is more appropriate. It is critical to have a focused research question – talk to your supervisor and see if you can narrow your topic even further. A good topic is one that asks something worth asking and that is answerable within 4000 words. Remember also that your topic should not be something that is taught in relatively good depth already in the syllabus (for example, if you are doing a specific English book in your A1 class, you cannot use the same book for your EE).

This is your perfect opportunity to research that little thing that you have always wondered about but that seemed too complicated to ask. Whether it be specific casino techniques to win at blackjack (mathematics) or Hitler's secret homoerotic sex life (history), find something that has great depth and actually interests you. Don't become one of those students who picks a topic that "sounds good" but has no real meaning – you will end up regretting it. If you pick a topic that actually interests you, then there is a greater chance that you will actually work on it! 4,000 words may be difficult if you are summarizing the Bible, but 4,000 words on your favourite television program seems a lot less demanding (DO NOT write about that). You may want to write outlines for several plausible topics, and then see which one would work best.

Another piece of advice about choosing an EE topic is to choose something that is relatively unknown. If your examiner has no clue as to what your topic is about, then you will be able to educate him/her; how much can the examiner criticize you if he/she knows nothing about it him/herself? And, as I said before, if you choose a topic for which you think you will find almost no information, you are in a much better situation than someone who has a multitude of sources from the go.

So how do you go about finding a final topic? Well, it will depend from subject to subject, but usually you will need something to inspire you. For this very reason, you need to start flipping through books concerned with the ideas you plan to write about. For example, if doing an EE in maths, I strongly recommend as a good starting point to look at a book about "100 greatest unsolved mathematical problems" and see if there is something there that interests you. Don't stress out yet! Just because it has not been solved doesn't mean that you will have to solve it! It just means that you can do a good research paper on it – find out what others have been writing and develop your own method at solving the problem. Try contacting some university-level professors and see what they have to say (this doesn't only apply to math, but also to history, economics, the sciences and so on).

The title of your essay (your topic question) does not necessarily have to be in question form. Nonetheless, the title is of incredible importance (see Assessment Criteria). You need to make sure it's precise, concise and clearly shows the focus of the essay. The sooner you get this done, the better – it will drive your essay in the right direction. Remember that the exact wording of your research question is not set in stone; you will be able to go back and modify it later on.

Time Management

Some schools suggest that you spend about 35 - 40 hours on your EE, the IBO suggests approximately 40 hours as well, other schools encourage 80 to 100 hours. No matter where you stand, you can see that a great deal of time will be spent on your essay, which is why you need to manage your time well. I was once amongst those who didn't understand why we had to follow a timeline for our EE and couldn't just do things in our own time. Well, I hate to admit it, but the timeline that the IB sets out ensures that you don't mess up and fall behind. This way, if there are any problems with your essay, they can be detected in the early stages, so that you don't waste your time writing an entire EE only to have it rejected.

Do yourself a favour and ignore any stories you hear from seniors who tell you how they wrote their EE in one sitting, a few days before it was due and got an A for it. Unless you have some magic ability to work productively non-stop for a good 80 hours or so, you will not be able to complete your EE in one sitting – or even in a few sittings. Take my word for it, taking small steps, one at a time, is the key to success. There are limits to this as well, however, so don't fool yourself into thinking that by adding a sentence or two to your essay you have done enough work for the week.

Your IB coordinator should ensure that you more or less follow the deadlines. Make sure you know all the important dates and keep them in your agenda (if you have one) or print them out and post them on your board. There will be dates for having your topic ready, finding your supervisor, getting your outline and bibliography ready and so on. Remember that if you risk falling behind on one of the dates, it could have a domino effect and some serious repercussions.

You will be writing your EE primarily outside of the classroom on your own time and, unlike with school homework, it is unlikely that there will be any check-ups to verify that you are doing the work. It is 'strongly recommended', but not 'required' that your school sets internal deadlines for the stages of completing your EE. Take some responsibility. I know that the workload in your other subjects will be heavy, but don't forget about your EE. I highly recommend finishing the bulk of it over the summer holidays (between IBY1 and IBY2). Also, I wouldn't rely too much on the dates that the coordinator "suggests" you follow – the more ambitious and independent of you should make your own agenda and stick to it. Set yourself specific goals, and if you fall behind, then make sure to catch up at the cost of perhaps even missing some schoolwork or failing a few tests (EE points are a lot more important than your everyday school work). Also, contrary to popular belief, working on your EE over the weekend is not a crime.

Supervision

Before you start writing your EE you will need to have a member of faculty "supervise" your EE so that there is someone to make sure you follow IB guidelines. Be quick and reserve your supervisor first because usually the more popular teachers are filled up with requests within a week – especially for the social science topics such as IB History and IB Economics. I strongly advise getting your subject teacher to be your supervisor because 1) they should know most of the material that the subject encompasses inside out and 2) they will be familiar with the IB program and will know what to expect. For your own good, try not to get a supervisor who does not teach the IB or who is unfamiliar with the demands of the program.

The role of the supervisor is very clear. They are strongly recommended to spend between 3 and 5 hours with you working on your EE. They are not there to write your essay for you, and you shouldn't protest against them for not helping you enough. There is a set of guidelines that supervisors must follow (once again, see IB documentation) in order to ensure that each student in every school gets an equal chance to maintain fairness. They are mainly there for support and encouragement, along with making sure that you keep up with the deadlines and don't plagiarize. They will also need to give you advice and guidance on undertaking research. The words "encouragement, support and reassurance" do not mean that they will write sentences for you. They will also decide on a set amount of time that they can devote to your EE (which is a good reason to choose a supervisor who doesn't have his/her hands full all the time).

Your supervisor is your friend. Remember that it is not an obligation for a teacher to supervise an EE – so make sure you don't abuse that privilege. Treat them like trash, and you will get trash in return. Don't be too demanding, but then again, don't let them get away from their promises. Once again, have a good read of what the IB suggests the supervisor does, and if your supervisor isn't up to standards, then you make the case to your coordinator to reach a solution.

I hate to say it, and this might come as an unfortunate shock to most of you, but I would say that your EE's success depends about 75% on your input, and 25% on your supervisor's. Although they don't actually write anything that goes into your essay or give you that much advice, the report that they submit to the examining board (which includes his/her personal comments) is incredibly important. Pick a clueless and incoherent supervisor and you will not only pay the price in terms of feedback, but also you risk having all the formalities that are involved with the submission of the EE to be incomplete. This is why I strongly suggest finding a supervisor who is confident with the IB Diploma system and who has at least a year or two of EE experience. I wish I could tell you that no matter how poor your supervisor is, you can still get an A, but due to the increasingly important role they play, this is not the case.

Look, let's be realistic. The more experience the teacher has with the IB and the EE, the more they will be able to offer in terms of what to do and what to best avoid. I know this is a problem in many schools that are just starting the IB program and where almost all the teachers have zero IB experience. But, if you have the opportunity to work with a teacher who has been teaching the subject for more than a few years, then I would strongly suggest you go for that. Trust me, you don't want to end up complaining about your new A-level accredited chemistry teacher just because he has no idea what an EE is in the first place.

Remember that it is your supervisor who has the final say on whether or not your essay will even get a passing grade. So if you choose a supervisor who is clueless about what a pass is, then you risk failing your entire IB diploma if your paper ends up not satisfying the examiners' requirements for a passing grade. Your supervisor should have you rewrite your paper if you are borderline passing (however, if you have been following this guide, this should not be the case!).

Find a teacher who will best match your subject and perhaps give you sources (books, websites, magazines, etc.) that others cannot. They need to be able to provide you with constructive criticism and guidance. Remember that you are not tied down to your supervisor with regards to help and advice. You can consult your seniors and friends for general

EE advice. If it is topic specific, then make sure you source the person in your bibliography. At the end of the day though, your supervisor is the one who needs to complete all the formalities that are described in the EE guide.

Getting Started / Research

There are few things in life that compare to looking at a blank page, struggling to come up with an eye-catching introduction. My best advice for you (and advice that is usually given to beginner writers) is simply to put the pen to paper and jot your ideas down. The introduction might not be the best place to start, so start jotting down your research in clear, coherent form, and eventually you will be able to start structuring your essay properly.

Your best bet before putting the pen to paper would be to conduct some serious research. Hopefully, your school will have given you a brief introduction into how to write a research paper, but there are a few things you need to keep in mind while researching. Depending on your topic, it could be that research is either incredibly easy or incredibly hard. The latter is probably the better situation to be in. For my EE, I wrote a paper on a 2,000-year-old mathematical riddle called "Alhazen's Problem." Googling it got me almost nowhere. Yes, I found some news articles here and there and some definitions and outlines, but in terms of raw research done, there was almost nothing. I didn't worry too much, because the internet (as great as it is) doesn't hold the answer to everything.

As an IB student, you need to learn to become very enquiring about what you are learning. There are several search engines designed specifically for research papers that you might need to consult (JSTOR, SSRN and Proquest to name a few). Yes, some are free, but some have a subscription fee. You need to figure out what it is you really want. Alternatively, you can try popping down to your local city library (because you've already gone to your school library, right?) and see if they have anything of interest. Be creative with your research. I remember having to email an Oxford professor to see if he could provide me with any information (unfortunately he totally ignored me!). Don't give up though, and keep in mind that all the other students are doing exactly what you should try and avoid. As great as Wikipedia, Bized and Dictionary.com are, you will not stand out amongst the crowd if your research does not go beyond that.

Whilst on the subject of research, make sure you take a look at as many EEs you can get your hands on in your subject area (preferably good ones). I don't mean read them through beginning to end, I'm just saying you may get some ideas about where to start once you see what a good EE is supposed to look like. The IB have now launched a collection of 50 great EE's (all of which were awarded a grade A) available in CD/DVD format for about a hundred dollars. Hopefully your school will buy a copy of this to keep in the library. If not, then try to get your hands on it by some other means (perhaps chipping in a fiver with twenty or so friends). It's not essential you look at many past EE's, but I would highly recommend it. By reading previous essays, you can identify common pitfalls as well as strengths in various topics.

39. Excel at the Extended Essay [Part III]

Structure

For most of you this will be the first time that you write an essay that has clear sections and a clearly defined structure. You should aim to provide a personal exploration of the topic and try your best to argue your points in a professional manner. Don't jump all over the place with arguments. Make sure at the end that you are able to make a contents page that will outline where you can find all the different sections.

I can't teach you in the space of a few paragraphs how to be able to write with good structure. That is something that comes with experience, good English teachers and a bit of luck. What I can tell you, however, is that unless you have some material to work with, structure will be even harder. If you have 4,000 words worth of material spread over 20 pages, then structuring becomes much less of a problem than if you have 400 words and no idea where you're going.

The main issue of structure will be writing the body of your essay, which should be presented in the form of a reasoned argument. You can choose to have sub-headings if this will help your readers navigate and understand your essay better. Do yourself a favour and stick to the IB guidelines. Find out exactly what your title page needs to contain, and make sure that you have no more, no less than what is required. The abstract also has very specific requirements that you need to look up, along with the main body, bibliography and conclusion. All of this information can be found right under your nose; the difference between you and the IB candidates who score more than you is that the latter will actually consult the IBO guide and use it to their advantage! Make sure you get all the basics correct, including your name and candidate number in the correct place on every page.

Constantly keep in mind how essential organization and structure of ideas actually is to your essay. You need to be very clear-cut and, please, avoid ambiguity at all costs. Remember that if you have clear sections, then you are already doing some of the work for your examiner in the sense that he/she will not have to waste time finding where your introduction/conclusion is.

Presentation

Make sure your final product is something that you can actually be proud of. No massive WordArt titles and colourful page borders, please. Pretend you are in university and are handing in your Doctorate. Make sure the paper is word-processed, double spaced, 12 point font (if you insist on using Comic Sans, then the IB is probably not for you), margins of standard size, and do not neglect to number the pages accurately. Make it look neat and not like some scribble that you rushed in the last few days. Have some logical presentation. It would probably be a good idea to number all of your graphs, maps and tables so that it's easier to refer to them in your text (only use diagrams and illustrations if they serve a purpose!). Even if what you have written in your EE is spectacular, if it looks like something that a five-year-old child scribbled out, then you have just wasted your time.

Word Count

You will almost definitely have a problem with your word count whilst writing your EE. Just make sure it is a problem of having too many words rather than too little. You're not in middle school anymore. Stop opening up "word count" to see how many words you have until you reach that dreaded 3,500 minimum limit, and then, to top it all off throw in another hundred or so words or lie and say you wrote 3,600 "just so the examiner doesn't think I'm an underachiever." You need to just sit and write and write and write until you feel like you have exhausted your topic. Cutting down will rarely be a problem, because you will have both "good" material and "poor" material on the page. Aim for 4,000, but don't make it *exactly* 4,000. Around 3,900 is ideal, really. For those of you wondering, "Why would I want to write any more than 3,500 if that is the set minimum?" –the short and honest truth is that 3,500 words could imply that the topic was not investigated thoroughly and you struggled to say any more.

Don't mess it up either. Find out and verify what is included in the word count (intro, body, conclusion, questions) and exactly what is not included (abstract, contents page, footnotes, title page). You will be penalized if you go over or under the limit, so save yourself the hassle and make sure you do your counting right. Essays containing more than 4,000 words will be subject to penalties and examiners are not expected to read and assess the material in excess of the limit.

Documents

Look, don't be stupid. The IB doesn't publish hundreds of pages of information and guidelines about the EE for no reason. READ IT. Believe me, the majority of students go on trusting their IB coordinator and EE supervisor alone, not even for a second thinking that it would probably be a good idea to read the EE instructions for themselves. Don't become one of these students. Get online, find all the relevant PDFs issued by the IBO that concern the EE and it would probably be a good idea to print them out as well. Highlight the relevant parts that you would probably not have noticed and consult the guidelines every once in a while.

You need to go to your IB coordinator and ask to see all relevant material provided by the IB with regards to the Extended Essay. It is a requirement for your school to ensure that your EE conforms to the regulations published in the official IB EE guide.

Assessment Criteria

Ok, read this very carefully: the grading criteria that the IB provides for your EE is undoubtedly the most important resource that you will use in completing your EE. The vast majority of students don't even know that such grading criteria exist. Don't be counted among them! Remember, although the method of assessment judges each student in relation to the criteria and not in relation to the work of other students, you are still in a way competing against the rest of the students writing an EE in your area, so you want to make sure you do positive things that they will probably forget to do. The most important of these is making sure your EE ticks all the boxes in the grading criteria, flawlessly.

The EE will be graded by examiners appointed by the IBO using a scale of a maximum of 36 points. This maximum score is made up of the total criterion levels available for each essay. Your EE will be scrutinized and the examiner will literally read each criterion, starting with level 0, until a level is reached that best describes the work being assessed.

As of the newer EE regulations that came into place, there is no distinction between 'general marks' and 'subject specific marks'. Now there is only the generic 'Assessment Criteria', however examiners are still suggested to consult further advice on interpreting the assessment criteria within the guidelines of each subject in the 'Details – subject specific' section of the IB published guide on the EE.

Now I'm not exaggerating. Once you think you have come somewhere near the completion of your EE, sit down, EE in one hand, Assessment Criteria in the other. Start with the first descriptor and go through each section. Give yourself what you honestly think you deserve in each part. The IB is very picky about their assessment of EEs. They will have someone sit down with your essay and do exactly as you are doing. Here's another fact you probably didn't know: they are paid by the paper. What this means is that they will want to get through each paper as fast as they can – use this to your benefit and make your essay more accessible for the examiner to mark.

This means paying extra close attention to the exact wording in the assessment criteria. If it says "the approach used to answer the research question..." then you better make sure you have the words "research question" somewhere in the beginning of your essay, and when you begin to answer it, make sure you say "the approach I will be using to answer my research question is..." I know, it sounds ridiculous, but believe me, you will gain points for small things like that. If they ask for an abstract that "states clearly the research question that was investigated, how the investigation was undertaken and the conclusion of the essay," then you damn well make sure it does! In fact, the abstract is probably the easiest section to score full marks on. If you read the guidelines, you literally cannot go wrong.

Get this into your head right now: the IB is not going to read your EE and give you a grade depending on how "good" your essay is. Even if you write a world-changing piece on a mathematical breakthrough, you must tick all the appropriate boxes in the Assessment Criteria. Similarly, if you write a pretty crap essay in your subject but manage to fulfil most of the requirements in the Assessment Criteria, then you will be surprised at how many marks you can get for simply following the guidelines.

The highest descriptors are not reserved for flawless essays, and if you deserve the highest mark then you will obtain it. There is no arithmetic relationship between the descriptor numbers – a level 4 is not necessarily twice as good as a level 2 performance. Moreover, it is also important to understand that scoring high in one criterion will not necessarily mean you will receive similar marks in the other descriptors.

Here is a great tip I learned from my own EE coordinator to make sure you get full marks in stating your topic question. Look carefully at the grading criterion part A, the research question. If you want full marks you need to make sure "the research question is clearly stated in the introduction and is sharply focused, making effective treatment possible within the word limit." Although I can't ensure that you fulfil the second part of that statement, with regards to the first part I have a great piece of advice for you. If you want your research question to stand out, why not make sure that in your introduction, you place your research question in a clearly bordered rectangular box, perhaps even shaded lightly. Use a bold font and place your question in quotations (see my EE if you still don't know what I mean). This could easily get you a mark or two (which might not seem like a lot out of 36), but you need to understand that if you work in a similar manner throughout the whole Assessment Criteria – probing every sentence and word that the IB use - you can easily pick up a few points here and there for just minor adjustments.

Although there is no longer a 'subject specific' grading criterion, you should not ignore the idea that your EE is specific to your subject. The IB still publishes subject specific 'details' which examiners will read before marking your essay. Have a good look at these documents because often there will be examiner reports and comments on common pitfalls and highlights of essays written in your subject.

If something is lacking in clarity or if you don't think you have met the requirements, then go back and make changes. Keep doing this until you believe you can get at least 90% on your EE – chances are you will be getting an A or a B. Be realistic when you are doing this and get it into your head: the Assessment Criteria is the most important factor in deciding how successful your EE will be!

As I briefly mentioned before, try and make life easier for your examiner. You don't want to waste his/her time if he/she can't tell where your introduction finishes and your essay body begins. Similarly, if your conclusion is muddled together with your evaluation (if you have one), then it becomes more difficult to grade. Although not obligatory, I would strongly recommend having sections (chapters) in your essay – that way you can expand your contents page to be more detailed.

The most successful essays written every year are done by students who have kept the Assessment Criteria as a poster up on their bedroom wall. If you know what the examiner wants, you can provide it for him/her. They will be able to skim through it and give you a good mark if you tick all the boxes that they want ticked. Bottom line (and I'm sorry for repeating myself, but this is crucial to your success): treat the Assessment Criteria as the key to getting your A-grade essay.

Sourcing

As the EE is a research paper, you would be foolish to leave your bibliography blank. In fact (and many teachers would probably disagree with me) you should ensure that you have a very wide range of sources and a lot of them. When the examiners look at your bibliography and see that you have consulted the good ol' Wikipedia here and there, Googled this and that, and stuck in a few sentences from your school textbook, they will not be impressed.

On the other hand, if you have magazine articles, dictionaries, real person interviews, university level texts, and newspaper articles in your bibliography, you're in a whole different league. Yes, it varies in difficulty from subject to subject, and depending on the topic, you might struggle to find even ten sources of information. That being said, don't be a parrot either and simply source everyone and everything you read. Collecting material that is not actually relevant to your research question is not recommended, as well as citing sources that are not actually used.

The other benefit from using book and paper sources is that they are reliable sources. By using the internet to do most of your research you risk quoting biased and sketchy information – be sceptical and read with a critical mind (like an IB student should!). Use your brain.

Also, you must ensure that your bibliography and method of sourcing is 100% in line with what the IB expects. There are a billion websites on the internet that will do the bibliography for you; some might even give you the footnotes/endnotes – just make sure you get this correct. You can use whichever system you prefer – whether it be an in-text system or a number system with footnotes – as long as you remain consistent. Just remember: you have to give credit if you are using someone else's work!

My own IB coordinator gave me an invaluable piece of advice when it comes to citing sources: when you find a useful source, drop everything you are doing and write down all the publication information (which you need for the bibliography) immediately on a set of note-cards. I thought it was a bit silly at first, but do this crucial step and you will thank me later on. When the time comes for you to actually formally write up your bibliography, you will have everything you need at your fingertips.

Another good reason to have proper citations is to eradicate any suspicion of plagiarism. Whilst small shortcomings in your referencing may cost you a mark or two, major problems could spell trouble for you in terms of plagiarism. Note any changes that have been recently made to the bibliography methods for the new EE's – notably that bibliographies now only have to list the sources you have cited and not the sources you have consulted.

40. Excel at the Extended Essay [Part IV]

Plagiarism

Simple. Don't do it. Yea ok, it's unethical, it's unfair, it's bad – all of that is true. More importantly, however, you will get caught. I have seen it all: plain copy and pasting off the Internet, the purchasing of essays for ridiculous amounts of money, and even getting specialist friends of your parents to write your paper for you. Even if the anti-plagiarism computer software (which has advanced incredibly over recent years) fails to catch you, it's your tutor's job to decide if the work is yours or not. Turn-it-in.com has been somewhat of a breakthrough in the way research papers are monitored these days. Keep in mind you will have to submit an electronic version of your EE – so spare yourself the drama and make sure you don't copy and paste.

I always say that the only person dumber than someone who knowingly plagiarises is the person who does it unknowingly. Fail to include a proper bibliography and cite certain sources "by accident" and you will taste the same consequences as the kid who did it on purpose. Don't make that mistake.

Now look, if you have been writing poor essays for as long as you can remember, and then all of a sudden you hand in a Doctorate-worthy masterpiece, flawlessly written and organized to perfection – your tutor (unless he's like you) will notice the sudden change in writing style and will question you extensively. Nothing looks worse than a student unable to answer simple questions about a paper he/she supposedly wrote. Reward is just not worth the risk, considering you are capable of producing something of a greater quality.

Come on now, it's only 4,000 words! Are you really telling me you are not able to write 4,000 words yourself without cheating and plagiarising? If that's the case, then good luck with university or whatever career you choose to pursue after high school.

Finished?

My teacher once said that your EE will never really be a finished product – there will simply come a time when you must hand it in. Keep this in mind whilst proofreading your essay and more importantly writing your conclusion. Please, under no circumstances write as your final sentence "In conclusion, there are .... The End" – the IB does not expect you to know every single detail about your topic and give a concrete and flawless answer. If you still have unanswered questions relating to the topic, then make sure you say so (and, if possible, suggest how you would, given more resources and time, go about answering these questions).

Now you think you're done? Well think again. Go back constantly and make sure you have done everything as best as you can. They are handing you an opportunity to get an A. This is not an exam for which you need to study; it is a piece of work that you can take as many hours as you need to complete. Go online and find an EE checklist, make sure you hit all the nails on the head before you hand in anything. If you're still convinced that you have completed your final draft, then I suggest you hold up your EE and ask yourself the following: is it something that I am proud of? Are you not embarrassed to read it? Is this your best work? If you can answer "yes" to the last question then you're probably ready to submit.

The Viva Voce

The IBO recommends supervisors and schools to conclude the EE process with a short interview, called the Viva Voce. It is a recommended conclusion to the extended essay process.

The point of the Viva Voce is to eradicate any suspicions of plagiarism as well as provide an opportunity to reflect on what has been learned from the experience. The whole interview will last 10 to 15 minutes and you should be ready to answer any questions your supervisor may have about your essay, including questions on specific sentences, citations, references but also on why you chose the topic, your high and low points of the process, and what interested you the most.

It may be possible that you won't have this interview, as it is not obligatory per se. Nonetheless, I would recommend you prepare yourself to answer questions about your methods, choice of topic, conclusion, and skills you learned during the process. Remember however that you will not be graded on this interview as there is no grading criterion for it and it's not compulsory.

To be honest, this interview should not pose any threat to the success of your EE. It is really just used as a way to catch students who are suspected of plagiarism off guard. Unless you have serious short-term memory loss, you will do fine. The process should end positively and is a nice conclusion to the completion of such a major piece of work.

Additional Resources

When I started the IB program, there was some material available on the Internet with regards to help with the EE. Now, having a quick look around, it seems as if there has been an incredible shift in interest and an increase in information with regards to the Diploma Program. This guide is supposed to help you survive the EE – but by all means, don't let your research end here. Make it your primary goal to gather as much information as you can. Find out what others are writing about the EE, ask your peers, keep Googling "Extended Essay help." No matter how hard I try, there's only so much I can put into this guide. You need to understand that there are hundreds, if not thousands, of good websites, books, and other resources out there that can complement this guide and your quest for more information. Keep checking the IBO website store to see if there is anything worth purchasing (or begging your school to purchase) with regards to the EE.

Don't exaggerate the difficulty and magnitude of the Extended Essay. Take it seriously, but don't get obsessed with it (if that makes any sense). Just remember what the real aim here is: to get an A or a B in order to boost your chances of getting all three bonus points. Three points is less than half of what just one of your courses can potentially give you (seven points). That being said, they are probably the easiest three points to obtain as there is no examination involved (so you can work your butt off and guarantee yourself the points). Don't make the EE more overwhelming than it really is.

Remember that if you mess up your EE, then you can wave two years of hard high school struggling bye-bye. It's not optional – it's mandatory. To be quite honest with you, after having completed the EE, I can understand why the IB would want you to write a 4,000-word essay. You won't find the same or any close equivalent in the A-level program or AP's, and if you go on to university, you will be able to separate the kids who did IB from the non-IB kids almost instantly by their ability to write long, well-structured essays. The EE, if written correctly, will give you a massive advantage later on in your further studies – trust me.

Since the IB suggests that the EE should take around 40 hours to complete, you could, in theory, leave the EE to the last weekend before it is due. There's a funny old saying about this extensive deferment of work – "the best way to get something done is to start it today." Start your EE the weekend it is assigned, finish it by end of Christmas break, and have it fully cleaned up and edited by end of Easter break – do that and you can take the rest of the time off laughing as your fellow IB peers continue to fool themselves.

41. Tackling TOK – The Essay

Boring. Useless. Naptime. "Wannabe philosophy" – just some of the words I have heard students use to address the TOK component of IB. My own opinion is not of importance, but let's just say I have felt very mixed feelings when it comes to Theory of Knowledge. As with many things in the IB Diploma, TOK has its upsides and downsides. The bad news first: it's controversial, at times utterly boring, and you might struggle to accept what the course is trying to teach. The good news: it's less work than the Extended Essay if you want an A grade and there is almost no academic ability involved. Whether you are an A student or an F student it doesn't matter – *anyone* can do reasonably well in TOK.

TOK is the only course taken by every IB diploma and certificate candidate around the world. The implications of this are immense. Your work is being compared to the other 200,000 or so IB kids taking it every year. So why do so many students hate the course? I don't really know where to start – it could be the lack of quality teachers, the "incompleteness" of the syllabus, or the fact that not a single other high school program being taught around the world has anything that even remotely compares to TOK. Moreover, it is frustrating for students how subjective the course can become. It can easily be the case that two teachers in the same school will teach and mark in completely different manners. The classes can become tedious as you start to find yourself questioning things such as your own existence and having endless repetitive debates about "how we know" something. The subject material found in TOK is mostly unfamiliar to both teachers and students, therefore making it all the more difficult to teach.

Out of all my classmates, I probably disagreed with the course more than anyone else (ironically getting the top grade for my essay/presentation). Get this into your head now: no matter how much you hate the course or disagree with it, it should have no impact on your ability to get a top mark. Yes, some will tell you that if you're positive and interested in the material then you will be more successful. This guide, however, will teach you exactly what to do (and what not to do) in order to succeed – regardless of your personal interest in TOK.

One of the reasons I find TOK so controversial is that some teachers insist on teaching TOK as the (ultimate) knowledge course. As if it's accepted worldwide that there are four Ways of Knowing and a concrete seven Areas of Knowledge. The fact of the matter is, outside your TOK class, no single other non-IB educated person will know what you're talking about. Philosophers have debated for millennia on knowledge issues and will continue to do so. It might be a sad truth, but the TOK diagram is almost "fictional" in the sense that it's made by the IB, for the IB. I'm not trying to take away the valuable lessons in knowledge that TOK does offer; however, I want you to understand that there is so much more depth and so many more interesting things to learn about knowledge outside the IB course. Just to show you how ambiguous and intangible the course is, in recent syllabuses the "perception" Way of Knowing has been replaced with "sense perception." This shouldn't concern you too much, but just keep in mind that whilst you are trying to ace your essay and presentation, there is much more to philosophy and knowledge than TOK tries to teach.

So what will it take? Well, the TOK component consists of a 1200–1600 word essay and a ten minute presentation. I have to admit that both are probably going to end up being extremely dull, but at least you should be happy about the fact that you will be getting very high marks.

The externally-moderated essay is worth 40 points (the presentation is worth only 20), which means that it has twice as much bearing on your final TOK grade. This is probably a good thing as it is externally assessed (no matter how much you irritated your TOK teacher throughout the years, he/she can't get revenge on you). You should be aiming realistically to get 30 – 35 points, which is not that easy. I have outlined several tips below that will guide you in the right direction.

The essay will require you to show your TOK assessment skills in a prescribed title that you probably would have never chosen if you could have come up with your own essay title. Examples will play a key role in your essay as well as a TOK-based analysis of those examples.

Half of the work in writing a good TOK essay involves choosing a good essay title. Out of the list of ten that the IBO provides, there will be one or two that have potentially more marks up for grabs than the others. Do not make the easy but fatal mistake of saying, "Ah, screw those long questions. The shorter the question the easier it is." I would actually argue the other way around. Shorter questions tend to carry a lot of ambiguity, whereas with longer questions, you know exactly what you are supposed to write about.

Look for questions that have a lot of TOK terminology in them and ones that will give you an opportunity to provide a lot of "interesting" TOK arguments. Remember that the essay will demonstrate your ability to link knowledge issues to Areas of Knowledge and Ways of Knowing. Don't go for the questions that you think are interesting to write about; instead, go for the questions you think your TOK teacher would find interesting to read. Anything that specifically asks you to compare, contrast, explain or describe an Area of Knowledge or Way of Knowing is much better than a question that lacks TOK material. If you don't think that the title suggests problems found in knowledge, then it is best to choose another one.

Take your time when choosing the title. Titles usually come out very early, and you usually don't need to make your final choice until your second year. Think long and hard about which question will allow you to demonstrate your TOK knowledge best and one that will let you critically assess. As a rule of thumb, the more TOK key words in the title, the better. Also, avoid questions that could have ambiguous meanings. Remember that you will be paying close attention to the terminology in the question and that you will be expected to address every aspect of the question.

Make sure you know exactly what you are being asked to do. Questions that require you to "evaluate" and "assess" a certain claim will require you to provide arguments for and against. Don't oversimplify the question and make sure to take into account all possible "grey areas." Furthermore, you need to understand every single word that is part of the question. You may think you know what is being asked, but make sure you look up different interpretations of the word (it's unlikely that you would include this in your writing, but at least you will be more prepared when you start writing).

If you're choosing a question that *kind of* sounds like something you could do a great essay on and you're hoping you can just edit the title just a tiny bit, well, think again. The title must be used exactly as given, without any form of alteration. If you fail to follow these instructions, you risk obtaining a failing or incomplete grade. Work with what you are given and focus on the title at hand.

Last but not least, don't be a sheep. Do not think that by choosing a topic that is more popular you will be able to get some good ideas from your friends doing the same topic. Since the essay is capped at 1600 words, there will be literally pages and pages of material to write about, which you will need to filter. Don't worry about not having good enough examples or arguments. And also, if you were to "borrow" an idea from a friend's essay that would probably be plagiarism anyways.

Where to start

My best advice to those who are just about to start writing their TOK essays would be to get your hands on as much official IB-TOK material as possible and highlight everything that is relevant to your essay. With TOK, you are limited with the information you can find on the Internet because the nature of the course is too specific. You can try Googling "perception as a way of knowing" and you will find two types of information – stuff written specifically for the IB TOK program, and stuff that other philosophers/writers have to say. Only the former is of any use to you. As you will find out later on, these "Areas of Knowledge" and "Ways of Knowing" are by no means world acknowledged. Only in the IB program will you find such specific classifications.

Nonetheless, do a fair amount of research on your topic within the realm of TOK. Hopefully your school has some TOK books lying around in cobwebs and dust – get those out and make notes on your question. This is the best type of resources, because they are written by the type of people who will be marking your exam – the true believers of TOK.

Unfortunately, you will have to be pretty good at convincing your examiner that you know what you are talking about. You need to show strong evidence of the Problems of Knowledge, Areas of Knowledge and Ways of Knowing. My best advice for you is to read the official IB TOK books that have been issued over the years. There is a lot of "fun" activities and rubbish in them, but you'd be surprised at how often you will find a quote here or there that will fit into your essay perfectly (of course not plagiarised).

Organization and Structure

My help here is going to be extremely limited. I'm sorry, but nothing I say will really make you write in a more structured manner or teach you how to organize your thoughts – it is something that you must learn and perfect over time. That being said, make sure you keep the essay title with you at all times on a separate piece of paper. Keep glancing at it from time to time and if you ever think a paragraph or sentence is simply too irrelevant, then take it out.

When you start the actual writing process, be sure to type out the question exactly as it is written, word for word, at the top of your paper (including the question number). Throw everything into quotations and in a bold font. This saves the examiner any confusion as to which question you are doing.

Your structure will largely depend on the nature of your question. If it is a simple compare and contrast between two Areas of Knowledge, then you could spend three or four paragraphs explaining how they are similar, and follow that up by the same treatment of how they differ, leaving a few paragraphs at the end for final analysis and conclusion. If you are asked specifically about different Areas of Knowledge, your approach may be to go through each one and explore how it relates to your topic question. Eventually you will end up forming some sort of concluding argument. Keep in mind that there is no single optimal way to write the essay, you need to use your judgement and decide what suits your essay best.

When your paper is complete, you should be able to read it and applaud yourself on your good transitions and structure. Have some rhythm and don't jump paragraph to paragraph talking about completely unrelated matters. If you are still struggling, consult an English book that guides you on how to have smooth transitional paragraphs.

Writing

The actual writing process should take far less time than the research and the post-writing procedures you have to go through. 1200 words is nothing really. As you would with the EE, try to push yourself closer to the 1600 target and further away from the minimum. If you have done your research and thought about the essay enough, writing it should not be an issue. Rarely will a 1200 word paper get a grade A – show the examiner that you are not a minimalist student.

Don't mess around when it comes to essay length. You can try and outsmart the IB by lying about the word count, however, that would be incredibly stupid as an electronic version is included. Remember that the word count includes the main parts of the essay along with any quotations. It does not include acknowledgements or references given in footnote form, or the bibliography. At the end of the essay, you should indicate your word count in bold to signal to your examiner that you followed the guidelines.

Your introduction should capture the reader's attention and summarize what the bulk of your essay will argue. Keep it short but well-written. Avoid any grossly meaningless opening statements and get into it straight away. Remember that you can't really afford to have a long introduction given the word count limitations, so be sure to establish your topic and provide clarity. Discuss the key concepts and include an insight into the major arguments of your essay. Also, while writing, keep in mind that it is probably best not to expand ideas too far – if you still have words to spare at the end, you can always go back and develop arguments in more depth.

As far as definitions are concerned, be rational. Don't give the Oxford Dictionary definition of "knowledge" – let about 10,000 other kids make this very mistake. You should know better than that. In fact, don't use the dictionary unless it's absolutely vital. When describing concepts such as "knowledge" or "proof," you are better off using the words of various intellectuals, coupled with your own interpretations rather than a wordy dictionary definition. Don't be fooled into thinking that by providing a definition, you have cleared up all ambiguities and complications associated with the concept – that would be stupid.

Some will tell you it's better to write a lot about a little instead of a little about a lot, whilst others will suggest you include as many TOK concepts as possible. The optimal, my experience has shown, is somewhere in between. If there is any specific terminology in the prescribed title then it should be clearly addressed and discussed in the essay. You do need to make sure you tick off an adequate number of Areas of Knowledge and Ways of Knowing, otherwise, the examiner will not know how comfortable you are with the course. At the same time the word limit will not allow you to go through each one by one. Filter out the best material to discuss. Don't sacrifice quality for quantity. If your essay lacks depth of analysis, your examiner will remember this shallowness in treatment when marking your essay. Clarity is the key – think and write clearly.

Some teachers may warn you against using "I" or "me" in an essay of this sort. This becomes very difficult to do when you discuss your personal experiences and your own beliefs. Try to get around this by avoiding amateur statements like "I believe that... I think that..." and replace them with statements like "judging from my personal experience.... Having witnessed something similar myself..." Catch my drift?

The conclusion is probably the best place to present your personal opinion. Here you are allowed to take a stand because you have already gone through all of the arguments and counterarguments in the body of your essay. Again, avoid being too narrow-minded and show an awareness of a variety of opinions. Also, if you haven't yet convinced your examiner by the time he gets to your conclusion that you have shown personal engagement, then at least you can achieve this in the last paragraph he/she will read.

Always go back and clean up your essay, making sure you have no elementary spelling and grammar mistakes. Although you will not get punished specifically for having any of that, it can potentially interfere with your structure and the "flow" of your essay.

Nothing Controversial

Ok, this is going to be very difficult to write, but it needs to be put out there. The name of the game is: tell them what they want to hear. Look, I know how you feel. It's that feeling of wanting to rip your hair out if you hear another person mention their WoKs or AoKs. Now, you can either be a rebel and fight the entire IB system and argue that all of this is complete nonsense. Or, you can be smarter and use this "flaw" within the course to your advantage.

I spent a good year or so arguing with my grade-eleven TOK teacher that much of what we are taught is simply the IB's attempt to implement an element of philosophy into the syllabus. I would sit there and laugh at questions such as "How do we know?" and "What is knowledge?" – I honestly found it a joke. Then eleventh grade came to an end. My teacher gave me a C for the year and marked my controversial mock oral presentation a pathetic seven out of twenty. I had to learn from my mistakes.

The lesson here is that you are not doing anyone a favour when you try to deny what TOK is trying to teach – you suffer, your classmates suffer, and your teacher will get fed up with you as well. I know it sounds horrible, but it's one of life's most valuable skills – the ability to tell people what they want to hear. You need to understand that you are only in this course for a few years, so you might as well suck it up and try to get through TOK as successfully as you can – whether you believe the material or not. That is what truly separates the top TOK student from the bottom. It's not what you know, it's what others think you know.

Here's an example. For my TOK essay I chose a title about the boundaries between various Areas of Knowledge and whether they are permanent. Initially, I wanted to argue that the AoKs are somewhat superficial, and that there exist tens if not hundreds of other methods of classifying knowledge areas into categories. Basically I was arguing that the Areas of Knowledge that we learn about are not exactly *correct* – they are simply an "IB" classification. After having a talk with my TOK teacher, it became clear that this was not going to sit well with most examiners. While I could have potentially written a wonderfully creative essay about various interpretations of the Areas of Knowledge and what other intellectuals believe, I would not score very high. I needed to focus on what the TOK syllabus is talking about - I needed to write in their language.

This is hard to swallow, I know. I'm not happy that it's this way, but there is little you can do to change it. Your best bet would be to just play along and outsmart everyone else. Leave your controversial arguments at home and get ready to talk a lot of TOK lingo in your essay. This includes avoiding bias at all costs. Even if you think your country/religion/sex/race or whatever is truly the best in the world – avoid saying so and keep it professional. Your essay needs to constantly focus on knowledge issues, no matter how non-TOK the essay title may seem.

While on the subject of controversial statements, another common pitfall for TOK students writing the essay is to make generalizations. "Muslims do this," "Americans eat that," "Women want this," – avoid making these oversimplifications. You should know that no two people are alike, so don't make false statements about a group/nationality/country that have no real basis except your own stereotyping. This just reeks of an anti-TOK way of thinking and you don't want the examiner to know that you are that close-minded. You are going against the whole IB concept of making you an open-minded individual. Be very careful when using words such as "all," "mostly" and "usually." To be fair, you are more likely to write these statements by accident, which is fine, as long as you can spot and rephrase them before you send off your essay.

Examples

The factor that will separate your essay from other students doing the same essay will be your use of examples. Now, this being the IB, you need to make sure your examples are personal, unique and ethically correct. You need examples from other cultures and countries, and they need to appear researched and not just made up.

One of the reasons I strongly suggest that you refrain from sleeping in your TOK class is because you might miss out on potentially good examples brought up by your classmates or teacher. Keep one eye open for anything that could be put into your essay. Go over your notes (if you bothered to make any) and remind yourself of some of the stuff that was discussed in class. Gather examples from newspapers, magazines, Internet or any other relevant source. You will need to filter this by throwing away the "poor" examples and carefully but rigorously summarizing the "good" examples.

Remember that you will be given credit in your essay for not only tying all the relevant ideas and arguments together, but also for drawing on your own life experiences and personal analysis. Make sure you throw in a few cultural and internationally diverse examples here and there. If you've lived in hundreds of different countries and speak ten languages, use that to your advantage. Include not only your own experience but also examples from other cultures with which you have become familiar. Your essay could end up in the hands of an examiner living anywhere from Poland to China. Use a wide variety of sources, but more importantly, make sure that they actually clearly portray the point that you are making. Avoid superficial examples that all high school students think of: Galileo, Francis Bacon's dictum, Inuit words for snow and embryonic stem cell research are worn-out examples – be original!

You will often be advised to find linkages in your IB subjects and you are encouraged to point out these connections. In the TOK essay this is also the case. If you are writing about something and then a little light bulb goes off in your head to tell you, "Hey, we actually discussed this in biology class," then make sure you mention that one way or another. You are likely to be reading great literary texts in your IB English class and learning about some of the most influential people in your history class, so why not see if there is any TOK-related stuff to talk about there.

As far as actual quotations go, I would not overestimate their importance. It's impressive to show the examiner that you appreciate what some of the greatest minds in the world have had to say about your topic, but another person's opinion is only worth so much. Use these more as a stylistic device, rather than as a method to prove a point. As a general rule, you can either start with a quote to set the mood or summarize with a quote to have a lasting and memorable impact on your reader.

As long as we are on the subject of examples, I would also warn you to avoid using examples which are not clearly connected to the topic in question. If you have included an example that you doubt has any real significant impact on the essay, then you're better off taking it out. Similarly, if you can't remember why you placed that example there, then it means it's not proving a point – take it out!

Marking Criteria

As with almost everything else that has assessment criteria in the IB program, the marking criteria is of the highest importance. Read the official IB instructions over and over again. Once you have come close to finishing your essay, sit down and pretend you are the examiner. Give yourself what you think you will get out of 40 points.

Do you have evidence to prove that you know enough about problems of knowledge and that you have experience as a "knower"? Have you included enough examples to illustrate your points? Have you answered the question as it is stated? Did you score 35+ points when you graded yourself against the assessment criteria? If you gave your essay to a fellow TOK student in your class, would he mark it +/- 35 points as well (something I recommend you do if you have helpful friends)?

Make sure you can answer yes to those questions. Pay extremely close attention to the descriptors for top marks in each category. Also, you should note that the first two categories give up to 10 potential marks (twice that of the other categories). For top marks in criteria A, Knowledge Issues, you must have "an excellent recognition and understanding of the problems of knowledge implied by the title" and your "development of ideas is consistently relevant to the prescribed title in particular, and to TOK in general." Does that sound like your essay? Can you get at least 7 or 8 points?

Take that type of approach for all of the different criteria. Some may be clearer than others. For example to score top marks under criteria D (Structure, Clarity and Logical Coherence), you need to have an essay that is "excellently structured, with a concise introduction, and a clear, logically coherent development of the arguments leading to an effective conclusion." So, even if you are a great essay writer and can structure your essay flawlessly, you might get all 5 marks in this category no matter how poor your TOK knowledge is.

Bibliography

Keep in mind that there is an actual grading criterion for your use of sourced material. In order to get all 5 marks in criterion F (Factual Accuracy and Reliability), you must have "an excellent level of factual accuracy, and sources that are reliable, consistently and correctly cited, according to a recognized convention." That is not asking too much of you. Make sure you cite all your work and use a well-known citation method to ensure your bibliography is 100% correct. Remember, even one mistake (such as misuse of quotation marks or italics in the bibliography listings) could cost you one or two marks.

I know it is perfectly feasible to write an entire TOK essay without consulting a single source. While I would normally tell you that this is OK – the fact that there is a specific grading criterion just for sourced material could spell trouble. Be on the safe side. Don't think, "Oh man, I don't have a single source, which means no bibliography, which means they have to give me all 5 marks, because there can't be any mistakes!" Unfortunately it doesn't work like that. There is still the possibility that you will lose marks for not having sources when you really should have. Do the wise thing and make the effort to include a proper bibliography. The IBO does warn that, "Essays which require facts to support the argument, but omit them, will be awarded zero." Don't take that risk.

Keep in mind this is not a research paper – the *Theory of Knowledge Guide* provided by the IB states that 'neither the [TOK] essay nor the presentation is primarily a research exercise'. Anything in excess of five sources for a 1600 word essay in TOK is a bit sketchy, because you are expected to rely on your own experiences and analysis more. Keep sources to a minimum but make sure you have something there. Please don't mess up and "accidently" forget to source an entire statement that you just ripped off from a newspaper article. You will probably get caught – and you will definitely feel dumb. That being said, if you don't bother to look up information, you take the risk of making statements that are clearly false. For example, if you can't exactly remember what year Columbus discovered America and write carelessly 1294 (instead of 1492) you risk losing a point or two for your lack of research (note: I highly recommend you DO NOT use that example). It's not a research paper, but if you do use specific sources, then please include a bibliography just as you would for the EE.

All the works that you consulted, whether it be online, book, journal or television, should be included in the bibliography.

There is no guarantee that you will get 40 marks out of 40. My advice is to aim for right about there, and hopefully you will end up with 35+ points. If you follow the directions and marking criteria, there is absolutely no way that you should be getting anything less than 30. Make sure you get the easy points and try your best for the harder ones.

42. Tackling TOK – The Presentation

Along with the compulsory externally-moderated TOK essay, every student in TOK must prepare an internally-moderated oral presentation which should last ten to fifteen minutes (for you, this means 14-15 minutes). There will also be a discussion period after you are done presenting. The TOK presentation is worth a total of 20 marks, which is half of what the essay is worth. In your presentation, you will need to be able to demonstrate an "understanding of knowledge at work" in a real world scenario. Although a presentation sounds like a fun and easy thing to do, there are many pitfalls that students come across. Hopefully the following guide will help you avoid them.

To be completely honest, I think it's unfair that an ambiguous and confusing task such as a TOK presentation falls into the hands of those who often tend to be inexperienced TOK teachers. How is someone, who is just as comfortable with the topic as you are, supposed to decide 40% of your final grade? Much of doing well on your presentation will, therefore, depend on you understanding how your teacher's assessment works and figuring out what interests them and how to use this to your advantage.

Alone or Together?

Simple. Alone. Look, take centre stage, take a deep breath and work independently instead of trusting someone else with your grades. Remember that if you work together, you will still be marked on your individual performance, rather than that of the group. So even if you chose Mr. TOK as your partner and stand around picking your nose while he dishes out grade A material for fifteen minutes, your personal grade will suffer.

By working together with someone else you will sometimes give off the impression that you didn't want to do the work yourself or that you felt working together would mean you would be required to talk less. The benefits of working with other students are group performances, added input of your partners, longer presentation – all of which means more depth and detail. The costs, however, are concerning. The focus will be off of you; if your partner screws up it will hurt your grade. Furthermore, you risk being overshadowed by your partner and most importantly the presentation loses its personal touch because it's no longer yours.

If you think that by working together you can handle larger topics more easily because you will have more than 20 minutes to present, then I suggest you change your presentation topic. Trying to be ambitious and handle large complicated and broad topics with two or three partners will only hurt your personal grade. It's absolutely fine to do a presentation by yourself as long as the topic isn't too general. Chances are that the majority of students in your class will opt to work together. However, if you look at the "brighter" students, they will probably all be working independently. This is because they know that this way they are more likely to get an A. Don't take the added risk of working with someone else and take your presentation into your own hands.

Topic Choice

OK, tricky question. You are given the ultimate freedom when it comes to choosing your TOK oral presentation topic. There are absolutely no boundaries as to what you can do and how you do it. Given these boundless criteria, it is astonishing how many students fall into the trap of choosing aged topics such as "media bias," "stem-cell research," "euthanasia," "same-sex marriage" and basically anything that seems as if it's stuffed with TOK. Do not make this mistake. Nobody wants to hear ten different presentations on stem-cell research, no matter how "different" they are!

Stay away from these traditional, yet troublesome topics. Not only is there too much to discuss, but you will also struggle to be able to fit TOK information into your presentation as well. I guarantee that more than half of your class will chose one of these more "popular" questions, but I also guarantee that you will score much higher if you choose something original and specific.

One of the reasons I strongly advise you to go to TOK class alert and not sleep through the whole hour is that you will miss out on valuable presentation/essay material. Whenever your TOK teacher brings up a news article or a story that he/she thinks is interesting for TOK, jot it down in big red ink. So much goes on in the world on a day-to-day basis that just smells of TOK material and yet you wouldn't normally associate with TOK.

For example, the TOK subject that I chose for my presentation was not particularly fascinating and did not fall into the cliché of TOK subjects done throughout the years. There was a news story that came out a few years back about how the state of Florida wanted to monitor the teaching of history classes in schools across the state. Potentially this meant that they could rewrite the textbooks and omit/exaggerate certain aspects of historical content. Also, this meant there was one ideal way to teach history – no ambiguity, no questions. Clearly this will send alarms ringing in the TOK headquarters – which is good news for your presentation, because you can spend a quarter of an hour explaining everything that is wrong. Other potentially good topics of interest could be "How can TOK be taught in strict Muslim countries without being biased?" or maybe even a presentation into how Wikipedia has changed what we believe to be knowledge.

The point I am trying to make is that you will be better off choosing a topic (preferably from the news) that deals a lot with controversy in knowledge and the problems of knowledge. The marking criterion specifically refers to a "contemporary issue." Remember that at the end of the day you will be making a presentation not just about your topic, but also about how your topic relates to the different Areas of Knowledge and Ways of Knowing. Do yourself a massive favour and find a topic that is original and that you know will be good to analyze from a TOK point of view.

The reason I knew about that Florida story was because my twelfth-grade TOK teacher (who was, hands down, the best TOK teacher I have ever seen) brought it up in a class. I immediately noted it down because I understood the relevance it had in the context of TOK. You need to do the same. No matter how bad your TOK teacher may be, chances are he/she is still doing some work. You spend two years with them, so they are bound to tell you something useful at least a few times during that period. If that still doesn't work, you will need to get yourself online and find a good story. Try to stay away from complex topics that will require a great deal of explanation but also avoid embryos/media bias/gays and so forth. Also, don't try anything too controversial and start showing pictures of dissected sexual organs or analyzing anti-Semitic Nazi propaganda in an inappropriate way. Shocking the audience and your teacher will not make your job of having a grade A presentation any easier.

Choosing something that is relatively specific, such as a news story, an article in a magazine or a scene from a movie is much more effective than picking something open-ended and vague such as the death penalty. This is probably the number one mistake that students make. They choose a topic that sounds appealing but is simply too broad and needs to be circumscribed. By choosing a topic that requires a lot of background knowledge and explanation you will forgo valuable time spent discussing the underlying knowledge issues. The most effective and high-scoring presentations deal with issues in which you wouldn't expect to find TOK aspects.

Method

You could make a poster. You could do a play-like performance with a few other friends. You could even do a high-tech PowerPoint presentation with smooth transitions and amazing special effects. Or, alternatively, you could grab a white-board marker and do a TOK presentation so simple and effective you will wonder why you didn't think of it yourself before.

Your critical analysis is what will get you the top grade for your presentation. From my experience, analysis is much more difficult to achieve when you have role play, or a staged interview, or even a short film. Remember that you are assessing and evaluating the problems of knowledge and methods involved in answering the question "How do we know?" So if you can manage to do all of that in a ten-minute performance or movie, along with exploring your topic's general background – well, good luck to you.

The key to success in your presentation is making sure you touch on all of the necessary TOK terminology and explanations. From my experience, the best way to do this is also the simplest. Forget making complicated posters (nobody has telescopic vision anyway), or having an Oscar-winning performance. All you need is to ask your teacher if you can use their whiteboard for the presentation.

What you need to do now is to separate the whiteboard into three sections. This will enable you to separate your introduction (which should briefly explain the situation) from your main treatment of the TOK issues and your conclusion. Leave the middle section the biggest (half the board) as you will need to write most here. Make sure you plan all of this out a few days before your actual presentation by making an A4 paper version.

On the left side of the board you will need to provide a brief background and introduction to your subject. Remember that this should take no longer than two or three minutes. You can just bullet-point some of the main points of your subject or story. What happened, when it happened, and why it happened are all questions that should be addressed. Keep in mind that you will not be awarded marks for a narration of the key facts and information. Cover the facts quickly and filter out any facts that do not enhance your presentation. If you are still struggling to explain the facts and background to your presentation in less than three minutes, then a solution could be to distribute a handout summary to your audience beforehand.

The middle section of the board is where you will score almost all of your marks. This is the bulk, the core of your presentation. Remember that your presentation must investigate and critically examine the Ways of Knowing and Areas of Knowledge within the context of your topic. Along with that, you will need to develop and highlight all of the possible controversies (Problems of Knowledge) and pull it all off as if you know what you are talking about. This is not an easy task, I must admit. But it is exactly why this method that I am sharing with you is almost unbeatable. You will need to have the TOK diagram on hand.

Now, you need to take a good few days or so to think exactly which Areas of Knowledge and which Ways of Knowing are strongly connected to your topic and how you could analyze them. On the whiteboard, you will now need to draw a relatively large "spider web" and have segments branching out. For example, one branch could deal with "Perception as a way of knowing" in the context of your topic. Another could deal with "Natural Sciences as an Area of Knowledge," again strongly linked to your topic. By the end, you should have a good six to ten branches that deal with separate AoK/WoK within the context of your topic. The most successful TOK student can flawlessly make links between AoKs and WoKs when doing the presentation or writing the essay.

I must warn you, however, do not look for something that is simply not there. The only thing worse than lacking any TOK material in your presentation is filling it with obviously poor material that makes it clear to your assessor that you are just trying to touch on every AoK/WoK without actually having a worthwhile analysis. Don't think you need to include ALL of the WoKs and link each, one by one, to the Ways of Knowing and then link it all up to your topic – that would be just silly. Nonetheless, get this into your head: your presentation must focus on knowledge issues and not the content of your topic (which you briefly discuss in the introduction). Deliberate use of and linkages between WoKs and AoKs are instrumental in a successful presentation.

This part of the presentation planning is the most difficult as you will, perhaps for the first time throughout your TOK experience, actually need to really think about the TOK syllabus and material. I can't exactly give you any general hints and tips on what to look for because this varies largely from topic to topic. However, don't underestimate the power of your TOK books and materials. For example, if doing a presentation on the right to perform euthanasia, you could start by looking up "euthanasia" in the Appendix of your TOK books to see what they have had to say about it. So many students forget that the best place to find more material to include in their presentation is not the internet; it's the TOK-IB ready books.

I can bet that more than half of your class will do TOK presentations that go a little something like this: pick a cliché unoriginal social controversy, explain why, when and where, then give arguments for and arguments against. Oh, and then a cheesy uninspired conclusion. This approach has absolutely nothing to do with TOK. Presentations filled with an overview and description do not score highly – and the scores of your fellow classmates will reflect that.

You should be spending at least eight to ten minutes on this core section of your presentation. Make yourself seem interested and honest when running through each of the TOK branches on your web diagram. The key to impressing the teacher (your assessor) is to show that you know all the TOK mumbo-jumbo and what it means in the context of your presentation. Therefore, it is essential you pay close attention to how you speak and project your voice to your audience. I know that there are no specific marking criteria for your oratory and persuasive skills, but trust me – the more you seem like you know what you are talking about, the better your presentation will be.

The final few minutes of your presentation should be spent on the final third of your board/poster - the conclusion. This doesn't need to be groundbreaking, nor does it have to be completely open-ended. There are a few vital things that you must mention, such as a roundup of the problems of knowledge and your personal response to them. Before all of that, however, you may wish to just briefly sum up what your whole presentation was all about.

Your conclusion should be both evaluative and conclusive. Discuss any questions you still have, or other ideas that have come into your mind in relation to your topic. A clever way to round off the presentation is with the question, "why is all of this important to TOK?" You can even ask that rhetorically to your audience. Make sure your answer is well thought-out and shows personal involvement as well as a relation to other areas. For example, for my presentation, I concluded that the Florida law will not only have immense consequences for History classes in Florida, but we as Europeans should strongly value our "right" to be allowed to read and evaluate different interpretations of history. Make your conclusion valuable and engaging to your audience.

This is the part of the presentation where you can reconcile different points of view and explain your own personal opinion on the matter. Don't be afraid to express yourself, and even if you are leaning towards one conclusion, point out any possible bias or problems with your conclusion.

Avoid the stereotypical "there are many points of view... none of which can be discounted... all of which have equal value," as this shows that you have failed to really analyze and think about the conclusion. Your conclusion needs to summarize what your presentation was about in a few sentences and also present some sort of a forward-looking view, perhaps the implication of your conclusion in the future. Make your final few statements the most powerful in your presentation.

Remember to plan your presentation out a few days before you are set to go. Have your whiteboard "plan" scaled down and drawn out on an A4 paper so that you know where each branch will be and what order to go in. You should probably bring along a few bullet-point note cards if your memory is not up to scratch. Don't fall into the trap of writing another TOK essay and simply reading it, sentence by sentence, to the class. This method of presentation will score very poor marks. A good presentation is never fully scripted, but is supported by a few keywords and note cards. Have a few points jotted down, glance at them once in a while, but mainly keep your eyes on the classroom/teacher.

Speaking and Rehearsing

Although there are no specific points awarded for method or engagement of the audience, you should ensure that your diction and oratory skills are fully exercised. Avoid big vocabulary and try to speak in a clear and coherent manner. I can't teach you how to be a good speaker, but you can definitely improve yourself with practice. Stress the key words by speaking louder, placing emphasis on the end of your important sentences, and adding emotion where applicable. Also, make sure you don't rush your speech and become difficult to understand.

Engaging and involving your audience is a must if you want a successful presentation. If you notice your classmates taking a nap during your presentation this is certainly not a good sign – no matter how "dull" the TOK jargon and content may be. You will need to learn how to present boring material in an interesting manner (sounds impossible, doesn't it?). Don't lecture. Walk around the class, use hand gestures. Whatever you do, just don't keep your eyes permanently locked onto your teacher. Even if you are not personally involved and interested in the topic, at least make an effort to pretend you are!

Marking Criteria

Just as you would have done for your TOK essay, you will need to thoroughly digest the assessment criteria set by the IBO for the presentation. You will need to familiarize yourself with it. No matter how great and moving your presentation will be, if you ignore the essentials required in the marking criteria, then you risk losing out on vital points. My advice to you would be to find the marking criteria that will be used for your year of assessment (because they have slightly changed over the years) and print it a week or so before your final presentation.

You will need to be very honest when "grading yourself." Be a strict grader and run down each section of the criteria, giving yourself a truthful assessment as you go along. There are 20 points up for grabs, and you should be aiming for all 20, because chances are you will lose a point or two that you didn't expect when your teacher actually marks your presentation. There are four sections in the criteria, almost all of which deal strictly with TOK jargon. This is why it is so important that your presentation is packed with TOK analysis. There are no extra marks awarded for visual aids nor will you score higher for having an interesting or engaging presentation. Get this into your head: you do not need any visual props to make your presentation more interesting. You don't want to be labelled by your teacher as "yet another PowerPoint presentation." We are no longer living in the 90s; PowerPoint will not score you extra marks for innovation. This is the reason that you should stick to having a simpler presentation method (such as the one I suggested) and centre all of your discussion around TOK issues.

Criterion A for the presentation asks you to "identify a knowledge issue that is clearly relevant to the real-life situation under consideration." If that sounds too simple to be true then let me ask you why do so many candidates fail to ever say, "The knowledge issue at the heart of my presentation is..." and go on to explain the relevance of it? This is what I mean when I say that too many students simply ignore the marking criteria. Your TOK teacher is probably going to be holding a clipboard with the criteria paper and checking away as you do your presentation. You need to really digest the marking criteria and make sure you use key words from it to "signal" to your assessor that you are fully aware of the criteria and are aiming for top marks.

Some parts of the criteria are a bit more ambiguous and you will need to use your common sense if you want to get the top mark. For example, criterion B, Treatment of Knowledge Issues, asks for the presentation to show "a good understanding of knowledge issues" in order to be worthy of the maximum 5 marks. Most of you will struggle to fully comprehend what is being asked of you here; however, if you follow my key steps in how to carry out your presentation, you should score fairly well in the Knowledge Issues and Knower's Perspective grades. Notice how nearly half of the marks available centre specifically around TOK issues, which backs up my point about making sure that most of your presentation is carried out with this in mind. You should be able to distinguish your strengths and weaknesses and then make an effort to improve on your weak spots.

I cannot stress this enough, but the marking criteria is once again of great importance. It's not as important as it was for the TOK essay (because it leaves a lot more room for imagination and is more vague); however, it still should serve as the basis for how you present. I'm not discouraging including interesting non-TOK discussions to make presentations livelier rather than a dull, TOK-based monologue, but do so at your own risk. You now know exactly what is required to get the top marks, so if you feel that you can do that as well as present in an original manner, then you can give it a try. By familiarizing yourself with the assessment criteria you will force yourself to focus on the knowledge issues at heart.

Presentation Documents

Filling in all of the presentation planning documents and presentation marking forms can be a boring task, but you should make sure that you put in maximum effort nonetheless. Remember that the only thing the IB will see from your presentation is the forms that you have filled out and your teacher's assessment of the presentation – this means that the forms are of great importance to you. Make sure that you describe the knowledge issues clearly and explain the aims of your presentation well enough for the IB to be able to understand. If, in the highly unlikely circumstance, your TOK teacher really screws you over and gives you a clearly biased and unfair grade, you may still have the chance to appeal – if you filled in your forms correctly and have a good case.

Referencing

As with the essay, the presentation is not intended to be a research exercise. However, you are 99% of the time going to require sourcing of some sort of factual information. To make sure that there are no questions raised over the reliability of your facts and figures, I highly suggest you make a bibliography of all the information you use. Do this on an A4 paper and do it in the same format as you would for your essay. After you're done with this simple task, print out as many copies as there are students in your class and distribute them before the start of your presentation. Oh, and don't forget a copy for your teacher!

That's pretty much it as far as the presentation is concerned. Remember that there is no general formula for having a grade-A presentation; however, if you follow most of my advice, I can almost guarantee that you will achieve 15 and above. Even if you choose your own unique presentation method but stick to the basic essentials provided in this guide, you will still have a high-quality presentation. Although the presentation is worth half as much as the essay, it's arguably more important because it is so much easier to score high marks. Your teacher will most likely be more generous than an IB examiner. Although I heard of many 20/20 presentations, I am yet to meet somebody who has scored above 38/40 on their essay. Just in case you somehow screwed up your essay, you might as well max out your marks on your presentation and pray for an A overall.

Teachers

There is no such thing as a TOK teacher. I am yet to see a school that hires a teacher to specifically teach TOK. Usually it is the English teacher, or the mathematics teacher, or some other poor soul who was kindly asked by the school to learn the TOK curriculum and teach it. I specifically remember one of my friends coming up to me and saying "This is ridiculous! He comes into class on the first day and you know what he says? 'I know just as much about Theory of Knowledge as you guys, so this will be a learning experience we will both engage in!" These may be familiar words for many of you, and it's nothing you should be too alarmed about.

Your TOK teacher does have specific responsibilities when it comes to your essay and presentation. For the essay, he/she should offer support, provide advice, ensure that plagiarism has not occurred and most importantly fill in the essay coversheet. You could consult your TOK teacher with regards to the essay title; however, they are not allowed to choose the title for you. It is also suggested that your TOK teacher goes over one draft before you submit your final copy, so ensure that your teacher doesn't forget about this.

You cannot hold your teacher accountable for being unable to fully teach the TOK syllabus. Chances are, they never really wanted to teach it in the first place. I would guess that about nine out of ten TOK teachers wish they didn't have to waste those hours every week. There are exceptions, of course. Those 10% of teachers who actually engage in the TOK course will truly open your eyes. Don't complain about your teacher just because he makes you guys watch "educational" movies every week on "TOK topics" and forces you to keep a "TOK journal" and makes you do other time-wasting work. There are thousands of other kids in your exact situation. Luckily for you, your TOK teacher doesn't need to be Mr. TOK in order for you to get your As. You do need to keep a healthy relationship as it is he/she who will be grading your presentation but that's pretty much it.

Resources

Certainly don't make the mistake of limiting your TOK research to this simple manual. There are some truly wonderful TOK websites out there. Some provide simple non-detailed hints and tips (like this book) whilst others actually focus on the TOK material. Make sure you spend a good weekend or two just bookmarking the sites you know you will need to refer to again. It's amazing how many former IB students have taken the time to post up their old notes and essays for the world to see. Be a good investigative TOK student and do some serious Googling for material that will help you write an excellent essay or complete an excellent presentation.

Some have even gone through the effort of making specific checklists for you to print out before you hand in your essay to make sure it's ready. Make sure to find some sample essays. Some have even been graded by actual TOK teachers – this will help you see where people make their mistakes. Reading a few will make a big difference.

As far as commercial resources are concerned, I can't really say much. In my school we had two different TOK books for anyone who was interested, so I never really bothered to see if there was anything better out there. Now, having a quick look around, I could find online at least six books authored specifically for the IB TOK class. My best advice for those of you who are interested in getting your hands on a TOK book would be to first contact your IB coordinator or TOK teacher to see if the school has a copy. If not, consult the IBO store and have a look at the TOK Course Companion that they offer. I don't know what it's like, but having read their Course Companion on other subjects, I doubt you will be disappointed.

Don't rush out to buy everything IB-related that you find on the Internet. Make sure you know that the author is experienced with the IB, and that the book is definitely TOK-based, not a philosophy book. Do explore what others have to offer, but at the end of the day, ask yourself whether you really need it or not.

What do I do in class?

You have to remember that it's not your weekly essays or mock presentations or class participation that will give you the three "extra points" for your IB Diploma – it's the assessment and assessment alone. This will be frowned upon by teachers, but it's the truth: you need to do the minimum amount to get by, focusing mainly on your essay and presentation. These are your priorities: 1 – the essay (worth 40 marks), 2 – the presentation (worth 20 marks) and 3 – your classwork/participation (worth nothing, really). This advice should not be stretched too far – you do need to take into account that your predicted grades are important. Your teachers could impose consequences on you if you lack respect for the class and most importantly you miss out on valuable essay/presentation material by sleeping through TOK.

Here's the bottom line: do the minimum amount of work in class to get by with passing grades and don't irritate your teacher. Start your essay and presentation as soon as you have enough information about it – don't force your teacher to tell you when to start. You don't need to be that "top" student who always answers the questions and hands all the work in on time. You need to be the smarter student and do only what is asked of you: a grade-A essay, and a grade-A presentation.

43. Conquering CAS

This chapter will be kept very short. If you are honestly struggling to get the hours that you need for CAS then I cannot do much for you except shake my head in disappointment. The good thing about CAS is that it gets everyone involved in the community, teaches students to be creative and aims to keep everyone in good health. The sad thing is: if you were really that concerned with community service, wouldn't you be doing it already, instead of being "rewarded" for it with CAS hours? However that is not our concern. Your aim is to get your hours and finish CAS as soon as you can (preferably in the middle of your first IB year) with minimal difficulty.

As part of your "core" IB requirements (which include the EE and TOK components) you are obliged to complete the CAS program. This means that you must achieve a set minimum amount of hours in each of the three components: Creativity, Action and Service.

Creativity:

Probably the 2nd easiest CAS component to fulfil. You don't need to be a young Mozart or Picasso to get your creativity hours. First and foremost, engage in school creativity activities. This includes any play productions, choirs, and art competitions. If that doesn't work out for you, do something independent for the school community. Design their website, make a new banner/poster to boost school spirit, teach younger students how to draw/Photoshop/act. It's pretty easy to get your hours for Creativity, just don't leave it too late.

Action:

This should be very straightforward. I know what it's like to be lazy and non-athletic more than anyone else, but even I managed to get my hours with absolute ease. I joined the school sports teams not only for the sportive factor but also simply because it was a lot of fun. If you go through high-school never having tried out for the football, basketball, swimming, volleyball, tennis or etrack and field teams then you are missing out on a lot of memorable experiences.

You can't honestly say that there is a struggle to find activities to fulfil your "Action" hours requirement. Even the non-athletic kids at my school somehow found their way to the local gym and at least lifted some weights or did some treadmill running. There is always some solution available.

Service

This is the problem area for most people. I don't think it's because we are all inherently selfish and egotistical, but it is perhaps more to do with a problem in finding service work. If your CAS coordinator (assuming your school has a CAS coordinator) is living up to the expectations then you should be able to get advice and opportunities via him/her. I know schools treat CAS and especially the service component in varying degrees of seriousness. Nonetheless, you need to ensure you did enough to make the IB moderator satisfied if your portfolio is sent off.

The type of service you do will largely depend on where you live, how comfortable you are being outdoors, how fluent you are in the domestic language, and a variety of other factors that would make it too difficult to give you any specific tasks. Like I said before, no one is asking you to create a charity overnight or clean oil spills and create peace in the Middle East. You just need to demonstrate that you care enough about the community and do the hours required.

CAS Coordinator

As aforementioned, the school's CAS coordinator will largely decide the success of your CAS program. When I did the IB, the CAS coordinator was wonderful. Not only did he make sure that everyone did what was required of them, he also made sure that those who tried to cheat the system were sufficiently punished. Your CAS coordinator will either be very engaging and hunt you down if you are lacking on the hours (for your own good of course) or he will be easy-going and let you decide what you want to do and when you want to do it. The latter approach is a bit too risky for my liking.

At the end of the day you just have to make the best of what you've got. If your CAS coordinator doesn't seem to care about whether you pass or not, then that just means you will have to work that little bit extra than the student who has a CAS coordinator who does everything for them. Having a poorly run CAS program is not a good enough reason for failing to meet the CAS component requirements.

Tips

Although my CAS advice lacks much detail, I can offer you a few words of advice on the CAS program in general.

Completion – make sure you complete the CAS program as early as possible. I'm not saying you give up on all creative, athletic and community related aspects of your life for the remainder of your IB experience, however it will be more beneficial for you to complete CAS as soon as possible. I was done with most of the CAS requirements before I stepped into 12th grade. This did require a lot of work to be done while I was in 11th grade (including many weekends working, and also a school trip to help paint/build a school in Morocco during Autumn break).

My IB coordinator offered the opportunity to begin CAS work as early as 10th grade (a year before IB began). Those who seized this opportunity were rewarded because they would have the entire last year of their IB without the CAS burden on their shoulders. I had friends who were being chased down for a good part of grade 12 and this stress reflected on their other IB work. The lesson here is that the sooner you finish CAS, the sooner you can start to worry about all the other work you have to juggle for the IB. Get this out of the way as soon as you can – even if that means working in hospitals and running marathons every weekend in your first few months of IB.

Writing the Portfolio

Make sure you keep a very clean and tidy track of all your CAS activities. For some activities that exceed a certain amount of hours you will be required to write up an evaluation. Do this as soon as you finish the work, otherwise you will just forget what you did. Keep all this information in a very safe place and don't lose it because there will come a day when your CAS coordinator will ask for it.

Faking It

Just don't do it. How bloody hard is it to legitimately do the hours? If you think you can forge your tennis coach's signature, then don't act too surprised when your CAS coordinator calls him up only to find out you never did the 10 hours of tennis lessons that you claimed. There's nothing more sneaky and self-centred then claiming you helped your community when really all you did was just cheat. You will probably get caught and feel guilty as you are made an example of in front of your friends. Just do the hours – it's really not that much to ask.

While on the subject of misconduct, please avoid asking for CAS hours when you know you didn't deserve them. This includes doing paid work, tasks for your family, favours for your friends, and any other clever ideas you might have to score some easy CAS hours. Examples include kids who lie about jogging at home and forge their parents' signatures, or those who claim to do unpaid work for their parent's company. Don't end up like this. Not only do you risk being caught, you're also better off just doing the hours and benefiting from the experience.

University

One massive advantage that you will have over other non-IB university applicants (and even job applicants) is that you can use your CAS experience to build up your CV/application. Community service looks great when applying to competitive universities, as do creative abilities and an athletic lifestyle. Make the most of your CAS program at school because it will be of great use in later life. Even in my current CV I still have elements of community service that I did during CAS.

For this very reason, I strongly suggest that you make full use of your CAS program and do service activities that are more attractive than others. For example, organizing a concert at the retirement home is a lot more eye-catching on your CV than handing out pamphlets or walking dogs. In fact any service work that requires engagement with people you would not normally work with is very impressive to universities and employers. For this reason you should ensure to do CAS service activities that actually mean something. Similarly, playing for the school football team is more effective than spending an hour a day at the gym because it shows that you can cooperate with others and work in a team. Choose activities that you might want to impress with later on in life.

Failure

If you fail your entire IB Diploma because you did not meet the CAS requirements then there is little hope for you. I have seen some of the worst IB candidates still manage to scrape through their CAS program so for you this definitely should not be a problem. Don't overestimate CAS as it really should not dominate your IB schedule. Then again, don't leave it as the last thing on your to-do list because it will harm your other IB work.

A lot of students dread CAS. I don't understand this. CAS allows you to have a positive impact on your community. I promise you that if you are dedicated and actually spend time once or twice a week on an activity that helps others around you, you will feel like a million bucks. People that simply study all the time can never get the best grades because they eventually burn out and feel too much stress. So it's important you actually do things you like or have interests in. You should treat CAS as that much needed oxygen that's saving you from drowning. Try to pursue activities that you are genuinely interested in and don't just volunteer so that you can submit some arbitrary number of hours to your advisor. Give value to the world, and you will be paid back handsomely in the long-term.

I know for a fact that playing football for the school team had a huge benefit on my life in the IB. After those practice sessions I felt better, my mood was elevated, and it's always nice to be away from books once in a while. What I'm trying to say is that CAS is actually a really, really good aspect of the IB. It turns us into more open-minded individuals and gives us time to pursue our passions.

44. Academic Dishonesty

If you have come here looking for ways to cheat on your exams then you are out of luck. It's not that I'm an extremely honourable and moral person (although I would like to think so) it's just that there is no point in cheating. The information I have provided so far in this book *is* in a way tricking the system without *actually* cheating. So you are technically not doing anything wrong, you are just abusing certain aspects in order to get a higher grade – something that any clever student would do naturally. It is one thing to plagiarize your essay, but it's a completely different matter to slightly "manipulate" your lab report data in order to get higher marks. This chapter won't give you the best tips on how to cheat. In fact it will do quite the opposite – it will tell you why most methods of cheating fail and what the consequences usually mean.

You have to be pretty stupid to follow a two year program only to then have your diploma taken away for academic malpractice. That's two years of your life practically wasted. If you fail the IB diploma because of cheating then you are pretty much screwed. Why risk two whole years of relatively demanding work so that you can bump your grade up a little bit? The risk is simply not worth the reward. It's even more redundant given that you can easily get a higher grade by simply following the guidelines set out in this book. No matter who you are, there is absolutely no reason for you to even think about cheating.

Although the IB originated in Switzerland, don't expect them to be very understanding, or "neutral". Any form of academic dishonesty is dealt with the utmost seriousness. The vast majority of the time when you are caught and reported you will lose your diploma. Not only does cheating carry serious risks but you will also put yourself under more pressure. The threat of being caught will make you underperform and provide an unnecessary distraction.

Plagiarism

Plagiarizing is probably the most common type of academic dishonesty found in the IB program. I'm not going to go into an in-depth discussion of what constitutes as plagiarism and how to cite – your school should have already shoved that down your throat. I merely want to explain to you what happens when you try to do it. Hopefully this way you will avoid "accidently" doing it and think twice before you complete any piece of work for the IB.

Many of you may have heard of the website turnitin.com. This website scans for plagiarism. Depending on what school you are in, you may have it that your teachers scan every single piece of work that you hand in electronically. For those of you that have no idea what I'm talking about let me explain. Turnitin.com (amongst many other more sophisticated websites) scans documents for any evidence of plagiarism. They take your words and check them across a multitude of various sources: websites, paid websites, written books, magazines, journals, etc. The program then composes a very in-depth report that specifies exactly how much of your document is plagiarized and to what degree.

These expensive plagiarism scanners that the IB use are growing in sophistication every year. Almost every possible essay-writing database is now listed, along with written books that have been made into e-books. Even if you paid ridiculous money for someone to custom write your Extended Essay, chances are the scanners at turnitin.com will catch it because they can afford to scan almost every database.

So what does all of this mean for you? This should be a wakeup call for those of you who are likely to plagiarize "unintentionally." I'm talking about those of you who thought it was ok to throw in a few sentences here and there from your textbook because it's not available online. Almost everything is now available online and turnitin.com will scan these archives.

The consequences for plagiarism will more than likely lead to you failing that specific piece of work, and, depending on the degree of plagiarism, maybe even your entire diploma. I trust that you realise the dishonest aspect of plagiarism and will refrain from trying. More importantly however, I want to warn you to make sure that you don't accidently and unintentionally plagiarize either. I know that sentence doesn't make much sense, but it's for your own good that you make sure that none of your work is anyone else's words. So please, think twice before you include any sentence that is clearly not your own.

Why in the world would you even contemplate cheating on the actual IB exam day? If you're at a respectable and honest IB school then chances are that your exam centre is going to have some of the most vigilant proctors making sure that your every breath and sneeze is natural. You and your fellow candidates are going to be like little sheep surrounded by a pack of wolves.

Even before you walk into the exam room your face will tell the whole story. Even the bravest of you that lack any conscience will struggle to conceal that nervous and tense look when you step into the room. Chances are that even before you actually begin to cheat you will get caught cheating. This paragraph (and probably chapter) only applies to a small proportion of candidates out there, but nonetheless it's important to get the message out there that cheating on the exams is near impossible – and stupid.

Almost anything you can think of has already been taken into account. Random pre-exam calculator checks, plastic see-though bags, no talking in the exam centre, assisted toilet breaks, only bottled water. For every cheating method there is already an answer. The only "cheating" left for you to do is to follow the legitimate advice and tips that I have been suggesting. On exam day the only thing you should be thinking of is the exam itself. Anything else on your mind will distract you from doing your best. The IB diploma is not some middle school exam where you can write the answers on the palm of your hand, or slip in a cheat sheet. This is one of the most prestigious and respected high school programs in the world and they are not about to let their reputation slip as a result of academic malpractice.

As long as we are on the subject of cheating, there is one final word of warning. With the recent rise in cell phone and internet use, it has become almost inevitable that students discuss exam questions and answers online and over the phone. Make sure you are not amongst them. Schools have begun paying incredible attention to this and I have heard of cases where students were tracked through Facebook or their cell phone and eventually stripped of their diploma because they broke several rules about revealing exam details before the examinations were completed worldwide.

Given that the IB is an international program there are small possibilities for the manipulation of time zones in order to get exam information. But again let me warn you. Schools have begun to monitor students' cell phone use before and after the examinations. Also more and more papers are being divided into several time zones. There's probably nothing worse than being fully ready for an examination only to turn the paper over and realise you have crammed the last hour on questions that are not there.

The message here is pretty crystal clear: don't even try to cheat during your IB program because you will more than likely get caught and there is very little benefit. You can achieve amazing results without needing to plagiarize or be dishonest.

Cheating will have severe repercussions for you later on in life. You can forget about going to any respectable university if your diploma is taken away because of academic dishonesty. Not only is it a burden on your academic future but it also has serious social and academic consequences.

45. Appeals and Re-takes

Once you receive your examination results one of three things will happen. You may get the grades you were expecting and get what was required for your university. In this ideal scenario your IB adventure is over, and you can finally move on. Alternatively, you may receive your results and find out that you *deservedly* fell short in a subject or two, or perhaps failed something, and as a result your first choice university offer is no longer an option. The final scenario is that you receive your results and find that there are a few subjects where you know you should have done better. You are shocked because, as things stand, you cannot get into your first choice university or perhaps even your backup choice. There are several options that you may choose to take, outlined below:

Appealing

I'll be honest with you. When I first got my IB results in June, I did not get into my first university of choice. I got 42 points but fell short in HL Mathematics because I got a 6 instead of the required 7. My offer from Oxford was 40+ points overall, with 7's in HL Mathematics and HL Economics. I wasn't too surprised because I knew if there was one subject where I might fall short, it was definitely maths. Nonetheless, as things stood, I was not going to get a place at Oxford. I called up my coordinator and told him the situation. He highly recommended I appeal not just the mathematics grade, but also the 6's I got in SL English and SL Physics. The logic behind this was that if I didn't go up in maths, then at least maybe Oxford would reconsider if I got 43 or 44 points overall.

After several weeks I was informed that my English and Physics grades would not improve. This was very disappointing because I felt that my English exams went perfectly and I had superb IA marks for both English and Physics. I felt like there was no chance that my maths grade would increase because first of all I was predicted a 5, and second of all because maths is a rather objective – there are right and wrong answers with little room for grey areas and errors by examiners . Well, I turned out mistaken. I received the news from my coordinator that the grade had gone up to a 7, so I had met my offer and got a total of 43 points.

The point of that little story is that you should not just try to appeal when you feel like you could have done better. Even in exams where you are 80% sure you cannot improve, it may be worthwhile appealing if your university choice is on the line. Of course this will come at a financial cost, but I would say that if it is affecting your future then the financial cost is worth it. Besides, if the grade does change you will be refunded the full amount. Would I have appealed if I got my first choice of university and could see no direct benefits of a higher IB score? Probably not. I would recommend appealing only if it will affect your university decisions.

Retakes

In the unlikely scenario that you completely mess up your IB exams there is always the option of re-taking them in November. I am not a big fan of this option for several reasons. First of all, re-taking in the winter exam session still means that you will miss out on a year of university unless you can find somewhere that starts after the winter break. If not, you would be better off repeating the year and sitting the examinations in May

Second of all, re-taking exams is only a good option if you genuinely think that things will change. There is no point in redoing the exams if your approach is the same. If something tragic happened that distracted you from performing at your level, then retakes can be a good opportunity for a second chance. If however, you failed to meet your targets because you did not prepare adequately, then chances are this will happen again during retakes.

For these reasons retakes should only be considered as the final resort. It goes without saying that if you missed a university offer by a small amount then you should first appeal your grades before you even consider retaking the exam.

Life After IB

The day of your last exam will be a day that you remember for a very long time. I finished my last exam more than 10 years ago and I still remember that day as if it was yesterday. It will be a strange feeling. You go from having no free time at all, to suddenly having the longest and most carefree summer of your life. When you walk out of that exam room, you will want to celebrate but you will also be so incredibly exhausted that I suggest you go home and hibernate.

The reason I wanted to write a quick chapter on this is because I have seen over the years an alarming number of students suffer almost from a kind of post-IB depression. In the sense that, they just don't know what to do with all this free time they have acquired. Students have even told me they feel like they don't have a purpose anymore, now that IB is finished. They feel empty inside and unsure about moving onto the next stage in life.

First off, know that what you're feeling is very normal. Even if your friends are not talking about it, there are tons of people reading this who feel much of what you feel. I felt it after most major milestones (high school, year by year in college, etc.). There are short-term and long-term things you should do, and I'll detail a few of them and why you should do them:

Exercise – even if you hate exercise, go take a walk. Go play tennis with a friend, or go swimming, or something. Do this at least 3-5 times per week, and you will soon find that you crave the activity. It will do wonders for your state of mind.
Get sunlight. It seems strange, but sunlight causes your body to release all sorts of things it needs, including neurotransmitters which regulate mood.

Read – you've spent the last two years reading mostly what others imposed on you, so you've built up some animosity toward reading. But you probably used to love it, and you can again (and it will make you healthier and happier). If you need suggestions, PM me.

Make others happy. Part of how we define our self-worth comes through service to others. So go make someone's day. Maybe you take a younger sibling to some activity they love. Take your dog for a walk. Go volunteer somewhere not because you need CAS, but because helping people makes you feel better.

Long term, you have goals and a plan. What are small steps you can take toward those goals now? Maybe you read a book or journal article for self-education. Maybe you work on a website. Maybe you browse the syllabi for the classes you're taking this fall and decide to start learning ahead of time?

On the positive side, I do still contend that in the vast majority of cases, life tends to get better after IB. By that I mean, the workload and the stress at university is, by and large, substantially less than the two years of IB. I say this as someone who went to supposedly the best university in the UK. I honestly felt that IB was more stressful and difficult than my three years at Oxford.

Keep yourself busy and try and have some carefree fun!

Conclusion

Just please remember grades do not define your self worth. Remember that this is all about learning and trying to do your best. I have so many regrets because I spent so much time alone in my study procrastinating work, not talking to my family and friends, and missing out on really great events that would have made my final year so special. There is always a way to achieve whatever you want in life so long as you are passionate about it, no matter what IB you get. Again, a number does not define you, no matter how important it seems right now. You are a beautiful, smart and capable of anything you set your mind to. Do your best and live life.

And my final piece of advice to you is this, there are days that are going to come where you're going to receive a result that you didn't expect, the important thing is to move on, right now, your marks don't matter a lot in the scheme of things, but they are a major indicator of how well you're doing. So if you fall, get up, dust yourself off, and just keep going.

IB is tough, but you got this.

Contributors

Do YOU want to contribute to the next edition of this book? We are always looking for talented and insightful IB students (current and alumni) to improve and add onto this book. For more information on publishing your IB material, please visit www.zouevpublishing.com, where you can find our other range of IB books also. We are also interested in obtaining individual chapters on subjects not yet addressed in this book, so don't hesitate to get in touch if you feel like you have something to contribute – we would be happy to collaborate.

For any questions or comments, please email us at zouev.publishing@gmail.com

Special Thanks

A special thanks to my parents, who always supported me in whatever I did.

Roman, thank you for being a great big brother and an awesome editor.

Ken and Lynn – you guys were the teacher highlight of my school years, thanks for all the support. Mr. Oberg – you made me enjoy mathematics, so thank you for that.

The app developers at Bear & Fox – thank you for making my vision for smartib a reality.

CPSIA information can be obtained
at www.ICGtesting.com
Printed in the USA
BVOW06s1045110917
494541BV00018B/284/P